CHILDREN'S ACTIVITY BIBLE

Children's Activity Bible

Published in 2018 by Kregel Children's Books, an imprint of Kregel Inc., 2450 Oak Industrial Drive NE, Grand Rapids MI 49505 USA

© 2014 Scandinavia Publishing House

Drejervej 15, DK 2400 Copenhagen NV, Denmark

Email: info@sph.as

www.sph.as

Illustrations: José Pérez Montero

Text: L. M. Alex

Activities and layout: Isabelle Gao

Graphic design: Gao Hanyu

Activity editor: Linda Vium

Scripture quotations marked CEV are from the Contemporary English Version. Copyright © 1991, 1992, 1995 by American Bible Society. Used by permission.

ISBN 978-0-8254-4587-3

Printed in China

CHILDREN'S ACTIVITY BIBLE

Bible stories retold by L. M. Alex

Illustrated by José Pérez Montero

KREGEL
CHILDREN'S BOOKS

Contents

THE OLD TESTAMENT

In the Beginning	8
God Brings Life	12
Adam and Eve	16
Two Brothers	20
God Calls on Noah	24
The Great Flood	28
Promise in a Rainbow	32
The Tower of Babel	36
Abraham and Sarah	40
Abraham's Great Big Family	44
A Coat of Many Colors	48
The Faith of Joseph	52
The Baby in a Basket	56
The Burning Bush	60
Journey Through the Sea	64
The Promised Land	68
Gideon Wants Proof	72
Samson the Strong	77
Ruth's Reward	80
The Shepherd Boy	84
David and Goliath	88
The Wisest King	92
Elijah the Prophet	96
Esther, Brave and Fair	100
The Lions' Den	104
Jonah and the Whale	108

THE NEW TESTAMENT

Mary and Joseph	114
A King Is Born	118
Three Wise Men	122
Fishers of Men	126
Love Your Enemy	130
The Loving Father	134
Water into Wine	138
The Miracles of Jesus	142
The Great Storm	146
The Endless Feast	150
Back from the Dead	155
Jesus Walks on Water	159
Let the Children Come	162
Hosanna to the King	166
The Last Supper	171
Soldiers at the Garden Gate	174
Peter Lies About Jesus	178
The Cross on the Hill	182
A Cave for a King	187
Jesus Is Alive	191
The Visitor	195
Cloud of Heaven	198
The Wicked Leader	202
Earthquake at the Jail	207
The Shipwreck	210
The World to Come	214
The Promise	219
Game Solutions	222

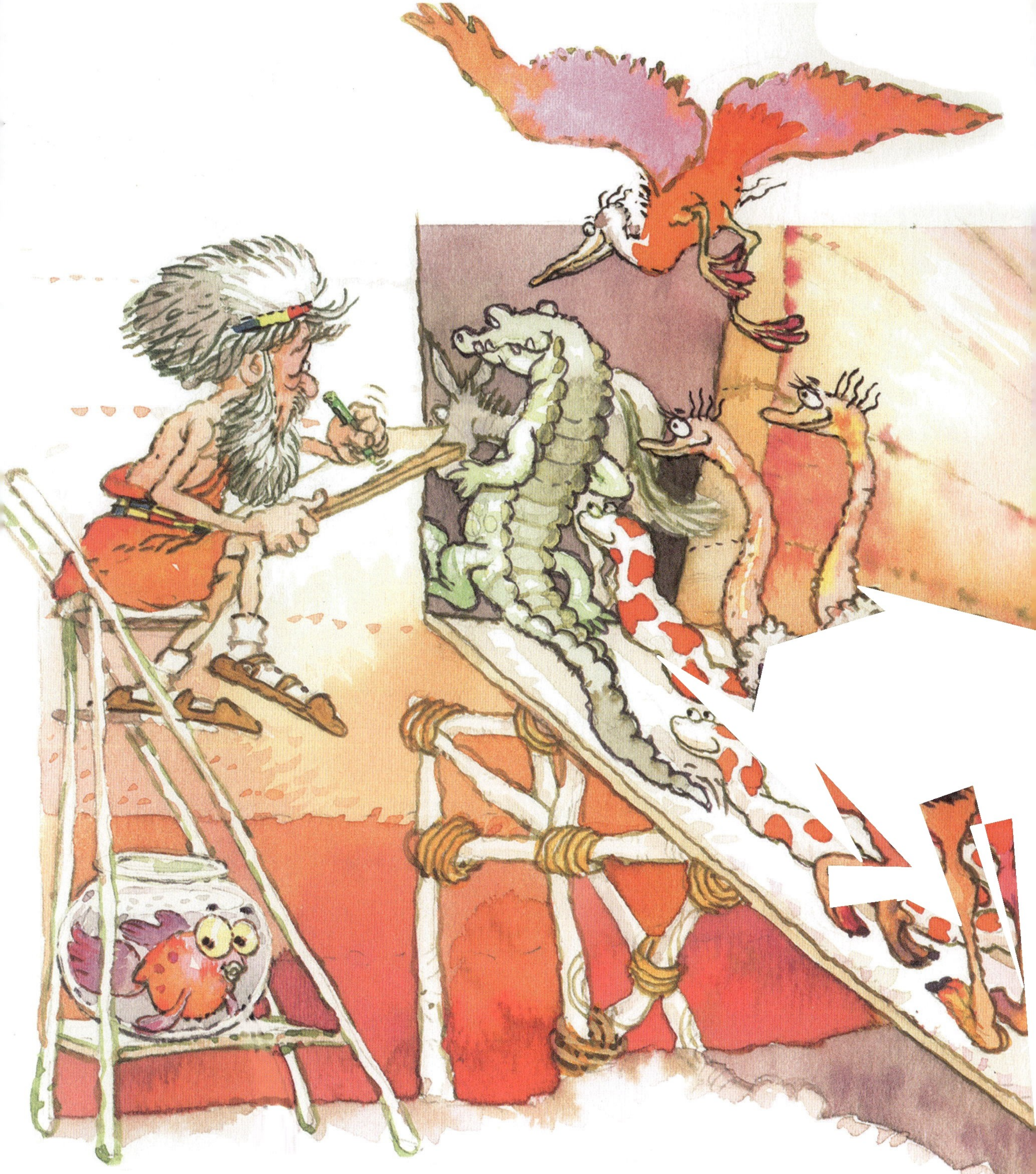

The Old Testament

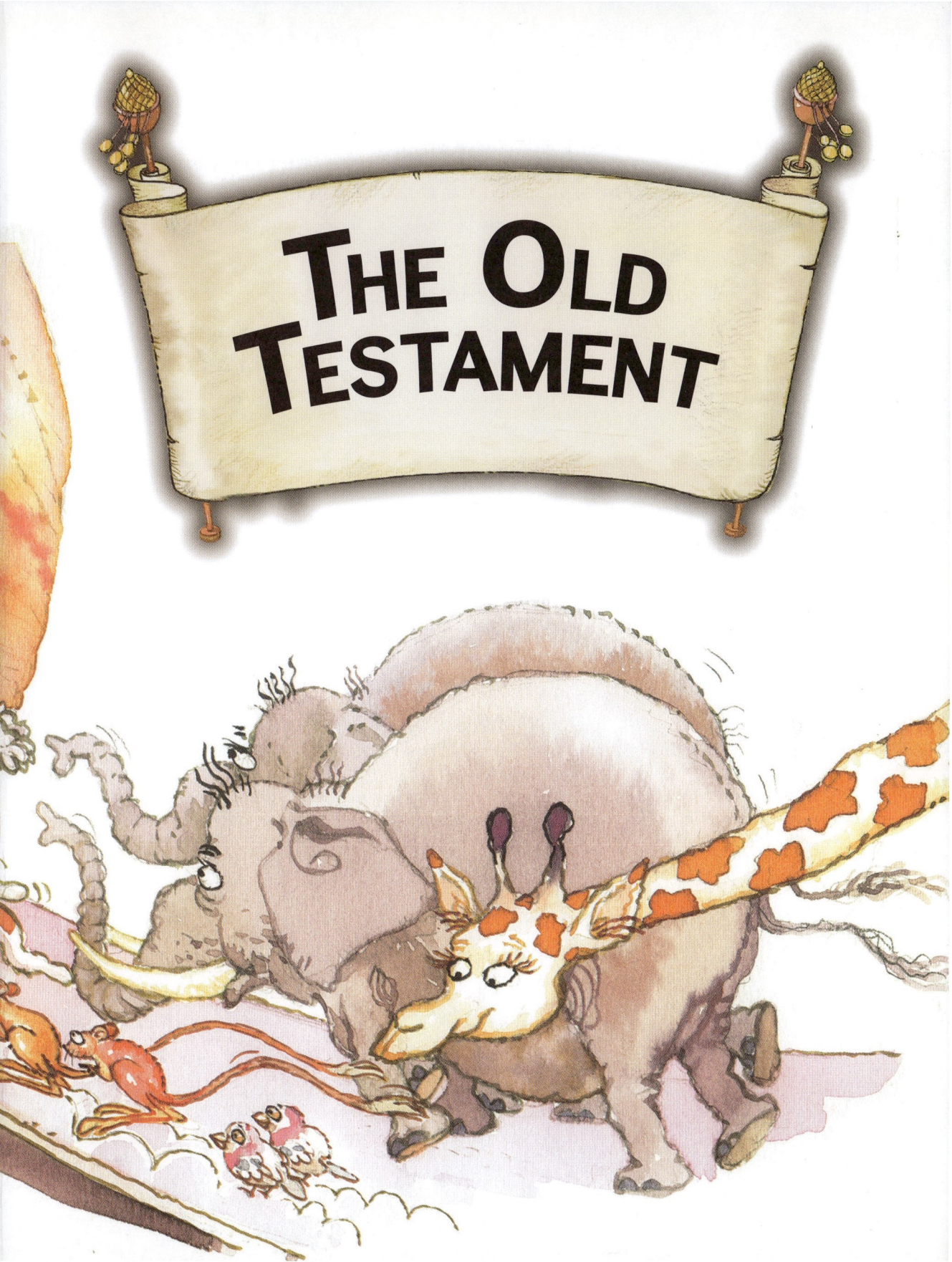

In the Beginning
Genesis 1:1-19

In the beginning, all was dark. But in the darkness, there was God.

God said, "Let there be light!" And there was light. God saw that the light was good. And with that, the first day passed.

God said, "Let there be an expanse for the sky." And so it was. On earth, there would be dry land, and there would be seas. A sun would shine for daytime. A moon would shine for night. And all across the sky, stars would sparkle, giving light to the earth.

God said, "Let there be lights high above the earth to separate the day from the night, and to count the days and the seasons and the years." And God saw that they were good.

Learn about the planets God created. First, unscramble the names of the 8 planets. Then, use the clues to solve the crossword puzzle.

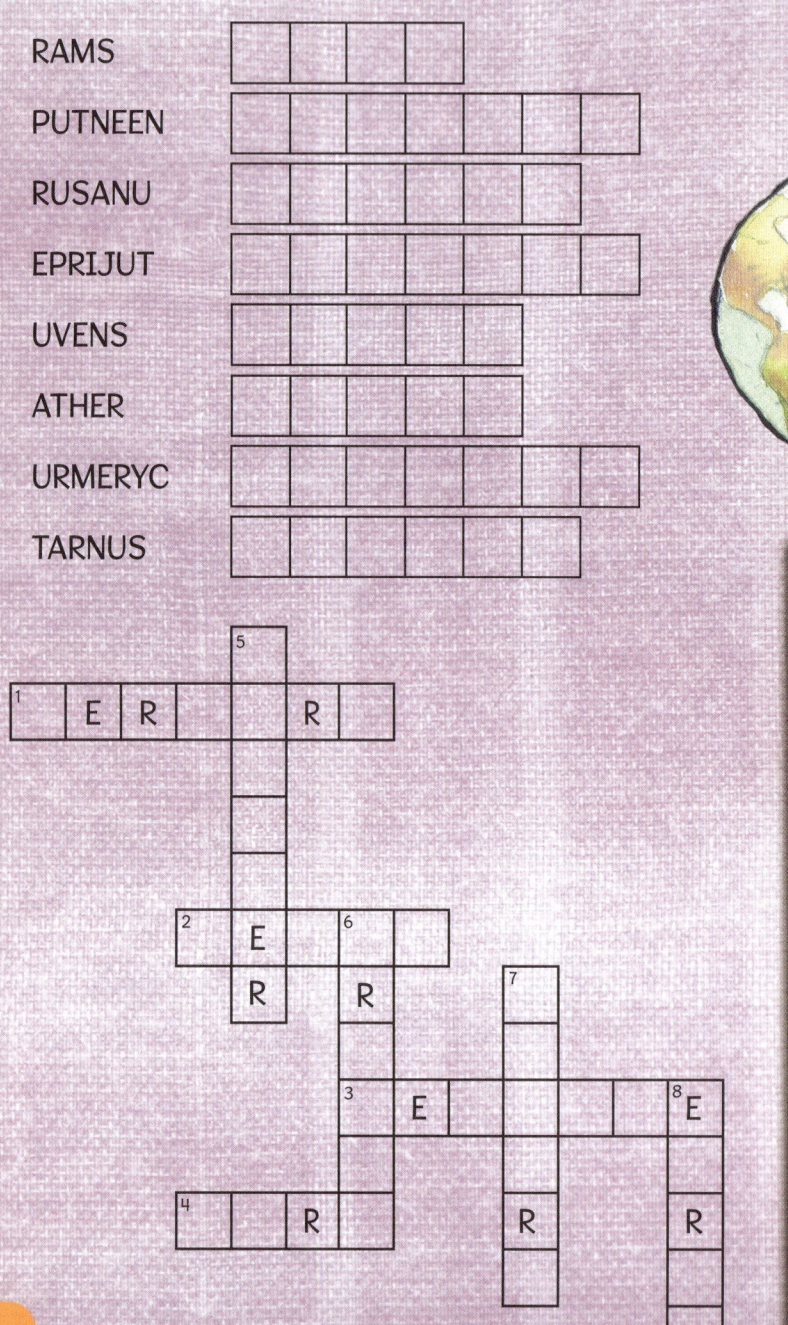

RAMS

PUTNEEN

RUSANU

EPRIJUT

UVENS

ATHER

URMERYC

TARNUS

word box
EARTH
JUPITER
MARS
MERCURY
NEPTUNE
SATURN
VENUS
URANUS

across
1. the smallest planet
2. the closest planet to Earth
3. the eighth and farthest planet from the sun in the solar system
4. often described as the "red planet"

down
5. the largest planet in our solar system
6. has the coldest planetary atmosphere in the solar system
7. planet with rings
8. the planet where we live

PLANETS' POSITIONS

Do you know where the planets are placed in the solar system? Fill in the letters for each name next to the planet. The letters U and R have been filled in for you.

_ _ _ U _

_ _ R _ U R _

_ _ R _ _

_ _ R _

_ U _ _ _ _ R

_ _ _ _ U _ _

_ _ _ _ U R _

U R _ _ _ _

God Brings Life
Genesis 1:20-25

God had made land, and God had made sea. All across the earth, plants would grow. Each plant would have seeds inside it for making more.

God made creatures to fill the seas, from giant whales that swam to tiny crabs that scuttled across the sand. God made birds to fill the skies. God made animals to live on land. Some would walk, some would slither, and some would creep. Each animal was made from God's imagination. Each was different, and each was beautiful.

God looked at all He had made, and He saw that it was good. He was almost done creating the world and everything in it . . .

"Be fruitful," God said to the animals He made. "Fill up the waters and the sky and the whole earth."

PENGUINS

Look at the penguins below. They are all the same except one. Can you find which one?

1 2 3 4

5 6 7 8

GOD MAKES THE ANIMALS

Can you fill in the blanks to complete the story of creation?

God created water and land on e _ _ _ _ .

He filled the oceans with f _ _ _ of amazing shapes and colors.

God made b _ _ _ _ to fly. Then He made a _ _ _ _ _ _ _ to live on land.

ANIMALS AND BIRDS

The names of the animals and birds were cut in half! Draw a line to put them back together.

1
- DOL • • BBIT
- ZE • • PHIN
- HOR • • BRA
- RA • • SE

2
- DON • • VER
- CHI • • KEY
- BEA • • MEL
- CA • • CKEN

3
- SNA • • TRICH
- PAN • • KE
- OS • • GUIN
- PEN • • DA

4
- TI • • COCK
- PEA • • GULL
- SEA • • GER
- TUR • • TLE

15

Adam and Eve
Genesis 1:26–3:24

God had one last creation: *people!* God made a man named Adam. God made a woman named Eve. Together, they were to take care of God's wonderful world.

Adam and Eve got to live in God's beautiful garden, called Eden. It was filled with all sorts of animals. It grew the loveliest trees.

Adam and Eve could eat fruit from any of the trees except one. They were not to eat from the tree at the middle of the garden. Yet one day, they disobeyed. They ate the fruit God had told them not to. So God would have to send them away. From now on, Adam and Eve would grow their own food.

Yet even still, God watched over them. And He still loved them.

THE ANIMALS GET NAMES

The animals all got names, one by one. Can you find 10 differences between these two pictures?

THE GARDEN OF EDEN

Find the 12 hidden words taken from the story of Adam and Eve. They may be up, down, across, backward, or diagonal.

```
G E F N E L W N A E
W A X C O K O B F N
O R R V E I A R K A
R T E D T D U N M M
L D O A E I E H B O
D E E R T N U N Y W
H R A N I M A L S U
C A S N A K E M Z E
B E A U T I F U L B
W D E Y E B O S I D
```

WORD BOX

animals	eden	man
beautiful	fruit	tree
creation	garden	woman
disobeyed	loved	world

Two Brothers
Genesis 4:1-16

Adam and Eve had made a home for themselves outside the garden. It was not long before God blessed them with children. They had one son named Cain and a second son named Abel.

Cain and Abel each had a special job. Cain was the farmer. He made sure all the crops grew nice and tall. His younger brother was the shepherd. Abel made sure that all the animals were taken care of.

Adam and Eve taught their children to give God thanks. All good things, after all, came from God. So, they gave God back a bit of the good things He had given to them. Cain offered God some of his crop. Abel offered some of his flock.

God likes Abel's gift more, Cain thought. Cain felt jealous. The feeling grew and grew until Cain decided to get rid of Abel. Cain killed his brother and then tried to hide the truth.

Yet nothing is a secret from God. Cain would have to pay for what he had done. Crops wouldn't grow for Cain anymore, and he would wander the world. Even still, God promised to keep Cain safe.

"If anyone hurts you," God promised Cain, "I will punish them seven times worse." God would even bless Cain with a family one day.

FIND THE LAMB

Help Abel find the lamb to offer to God. On the way, collect the letters and write them down in order to find out the word that means "to offer something precious."

The word is: sacrifi

22

ABEL THE SHEPHERD

Abel wanted to give his very best to God, so Abel gave the first lamb of his flock. How many times can you find the word LAMB in this grid? It can be up, down, across, backward, and diagonally.

L	L	🐾	L	L
B	A	A	A	B
🐾	M	M	M	🐾
B	B	A	B	B
🐾	L	🐾	L	🐾

The word "lamb" can be found _____ times.

The Good Shepherd

God is like a good shepherd. He knows us, leads us, protects us, and keeps us from harm.

God Calls on Noah
Genesis 6:5-22

The world had become evil. Gradually, the people turned to sin until everyone's thoughts were only wicked. Everyone except Noah.

Noah loved God more than anything on earth. And whatever God told Him, Noah would do. "I want you to build a big boat," God told Noah, "because I am starting the world over again with you and your family."

The boat was built in just the way God wanted. Then Noah and his family loaded the animals onto the boat. Two by two they went . . . those that slithered and those that creeped, those that flew and those that hopped. There was room for every sort, each in its place.

"Take aboard every animal," said God to Noah, "those that fly and creep and walk. Keep them alive for the new world to come."

Noah gathered up all the animals, including birds. Use the grid to help you draw one of the birds, square by square. Then you can color it.

Complete the puzzle with the names of the animals listed below.

CAMEL   MONKEY   LION   SHEEP   GIRAFFE

CROCODILE   ELEPHANT   OSTRICH   KANGAROO   GOAT

OWL   RHINOCEROS   CHICKEN   SNAKE   BUTTERFLY

27

The Great Flood
Genesis 7:11—8:12

The last of the animals had been loaded on board, and Noah's family went inside. God shut the heavy ark door tightly with a loud boom. *Drip, drip, drip.* It began to rain.

It rained and it rained for forty days straight. It rained until the whole earth was covered.

At last, the rain stopped. They peeked outside. There was nothing to see except water. The ark was floating on an endless sea.

Noah sent a dove to look for dry land. The dove came back once. It came back twice. But the third time . . . what was that in its beak? A twig of green—the earth was becoming dry! When the dove didn't come back again, Noah knew it had found a home. And that very soon, the rest of them would as well.

Noah built an ark, which is a very large boat. Find 2 compound words ending in the word BOAT. The picture is there to help you.

_ _ _ _ BOAT

_ _ _ BOAT

How many boats can you find in the drawing below? _____

MAZE

The dove left the ark in search of land. Help the dove find the tree.

STORY QUIZ

Try to answer the following questions:

1. How many days did it rain?

2. What bird did Noah send out to look for dry land?

Promise in a Rainbow
Genesis 8:13—9:17

Noah and his wife and Noah's sons and their wives all came out of the ark. What a feeling to be back on land! The animals went leaping and tumbling into the sweet grass of spring.

God had done all He had promised. He had kept all on board safe and sound. He had given them a fresh, new world.

How great God was! How much He must love them! Noah built an altar and gave thanks to God. On the altar, Noah laid sweet gifts for God.

God gave a gift as well. There above them gleamed ribbons of color . . . red and yellow, green and blue. This was the very first rainbow. God gave it as a promise that He would never flood the whole earth again.

God said, "The rainbow is a sign to be seen through all of time as a reminder that never again will water destroy the earth. That is a promise between Me and all life on earth."

WORD SEARCH

Find the 14 hidden words related to the story of God's promise for Noah. They can be found up, down, across, backward, and diagonally.

```
L U H E U F U N E X G P
H I S R D F L E R S N R
E M E U S E O O E M I A
H J R T B E M L O Y R I
A G F A R L S A Y D P S
L R N E I I N T T S E
T S T R N N L D K U T S
A I H G M G B Y D I A O
R G J I F T N O B B I R
Q N W F I E P G W S F O
P U T T W E V O O S I X
R A M Q D W S C O L O R
P R O M I S E E H B O T
```

WORD BOX

altar	gift	ribbon
color	land	sign
feeling	praises	spring
flood	promise	sweet
fresh	rainbow	

WHAT IS DIFFERENT?

Can you find 10 differences between each set of pictures?

35

The Tower of Babel

Genesis 10:32—11:9

People built up towns. The towns turned into cities. Soon people got to thinking they were mightier than God. "Why wait on God?" said one neighbor to another. "We could build a tower to heaven and climb there ourselves."

The plan was set in motion. Brick by brick, the tower rose high.

God saw everything. And easier than they could build it, God could bring it down.

God decided to bring down the proud way they thought about themselves instead. All of a sudden, every builder spoke a different language. Each thought it was the other who was speaking gibberish. No one could understand one another. No one could cooperate. So they scattered all over the earth.

"You were so proud," says God, "that you got yourself tricked. You built your place up high like you were some mighty eagle. You said to yourself, 'Who can bring me down?' I will bring you down," says God, "for all your wicked deeds."

THE TOWER

Follow the line for each letter to find out where the letter goes.

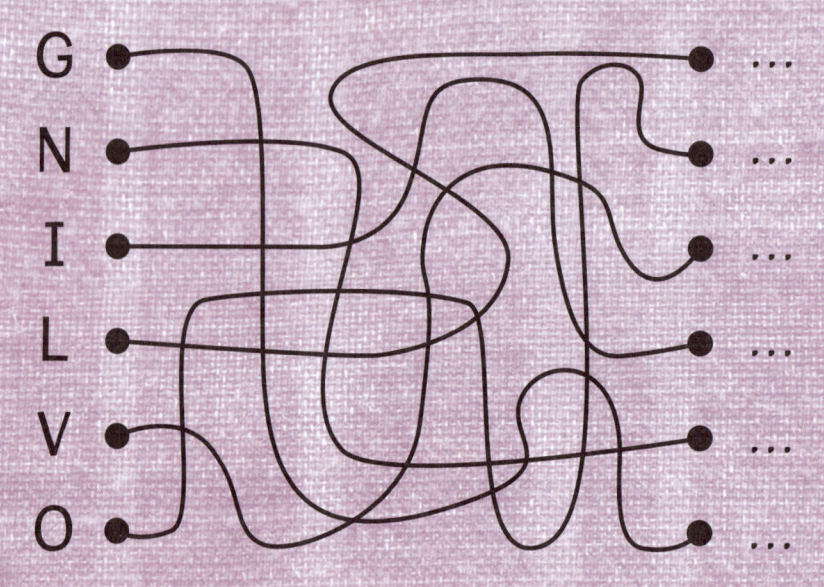

G
N
I
L
V
O

One of these towers is different. Can you circle it?

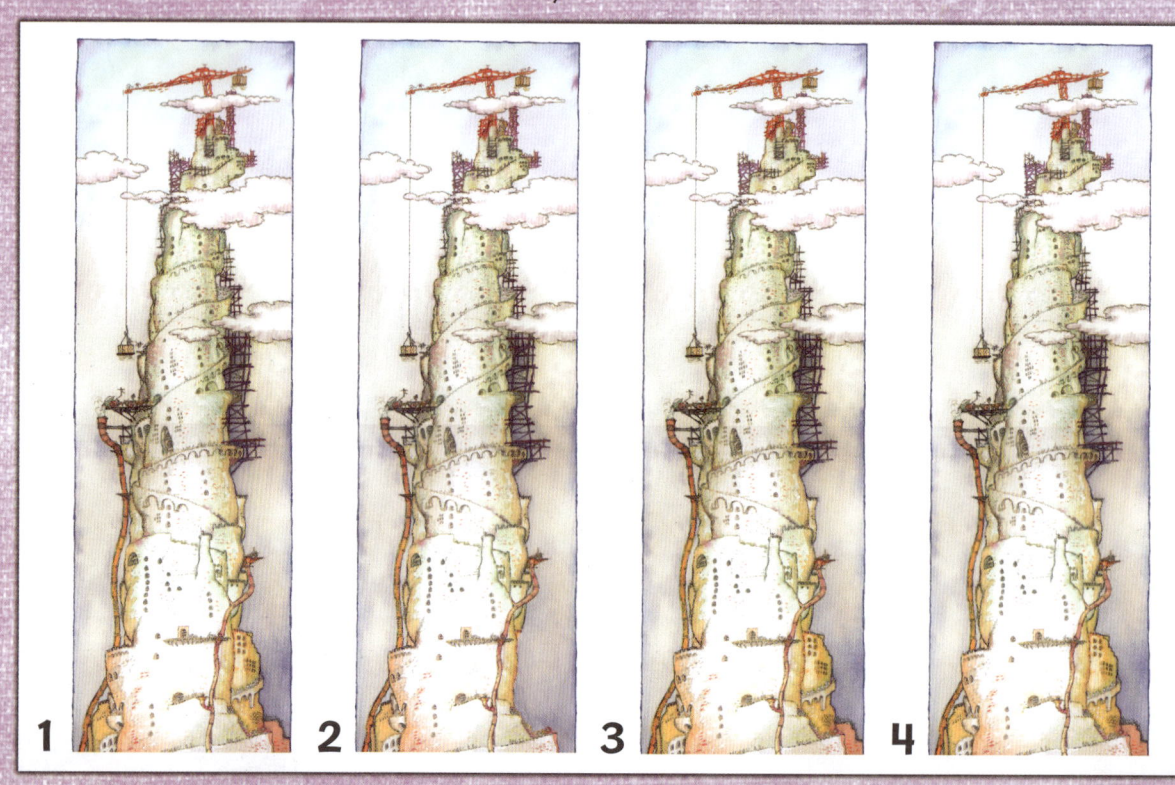

1   2   3   4

LANGUAGES & COUNTRIES

God punished the people of Babel by giving them each their own language. Today, people live in many different countries speaking their own languages.

Where are you from? Can you find your country on the map?

Can you also find on the map:
1. the boy with blond hair wearing the white and red sweater
2. the Mexican boy with a hat and a striped scarf
3. the Japanese lady with an umbrella
4. the Aboriginal Australian boy holding a spear

Abraham and Sarah
Genesis 12–13, 15

"Yes," said Abraham and Sarah. They would go anywhere that God told them to go. No journey would be too long if it was God's plan.

They would even sleep in a tent. They would camp out in the desert as long as God wanted. When things felt less than comfy, they remained content. They knew that God was always planning good things for the faithful.

What they did not know was that God's plan was better than they could even imagine. He had sent them away to bring them to a better home, to build a new nation . . . that would all begin with them.

"Look up at the sky," God told Abraham. "Do you see all the stars above?" asked God. "Your family will one day be as many as the stars, as many as the grains of sand on the seashore."

41

A LONG JOURNEY

Can you find and circle these things in the picture?

1. a dog
2. a grey goat
3. a mouse wearing pants
4. a suitcase with a flower
5. a frying pan
6. a red bell

DID YOU KNOW?

Abraham (Abram) is a descendant of Shem, son of Noah. Noah was still alive when Abraham was born.

A NOMAD'S LIFE

Help Abraham find the oasis in the desert. You need to avoid the dangers on the way!

Synonyms are words that have the same meaning. Draw a line to connect the synonyms together.

LAND	CAMP
SHELTER	WILDERNESS
PROMISE	VOW
TRUST	COUNTRY
DESERT	FAITH

43

Abraham's Great Big Family
Genesis 17; 18:1-15; 21:1-8

What God had promised, God would do. And He had promised a great big family to Sarah and Abraham. Sometimes the two doubted and worried when they had no child. But God always had a plan.

Abraham and Sarah waited. And waited. They waited so long that their hair turned gray.

One day, some angels in disguise came by. The visitors said that Abraham and Sarah would soon have a child.

Sarah laughed out loud. Who ever heard of two old folks having a baby? Yet sure enough, it happened. Baby Isaac was the start of a great big family for Abraham and Sarah.

"Lift up your eyes," God said to Abraham. "Look north and look south. Look east and look west. All the land that you see, I will fill with your people."

ABRAHAM AND HIS FAMILY

From Abraham to Jacob

ABRAHAM   SARAH

ISAAC    REBEKAH

JACOB

Each description is about someone from Abraham's closest family. Read the descriptions carefully and write down to whom they belong.

_ _ _ _ _
was the wife of Abraham and the mother of Isaac. Her name was originally Sarai. The new name God gave her means "princess."

_ _ _ _ _
was the only son Abraham and Sarah had, and he was the father of Jacob and Esau.

_ _ _ _ _
He was the son of Isaac and Rebekah. He had 13 children: 12 sons and one daughter. One of them was Joseph, who later became ruler of Egypt.

_ _ _ _ _ _ _
means "father of many nations." At first his name was Abram (father is exalted), but God changed it.

THE VISITORS

Can you find 10 differences between these two pictures?

A Coat of Many Colors
Genesis 37

It was a lovely coat indeed. And it proved what the brothers had always feared—that their father loved Joseph the most. Joseph was their little brother, who bragged about dreams of the future and said they would one day bow down to him.

It was time for Joseph to learn his lesson, the brothers decided. So they sold him to a group of traders who were heading to Egypt, a faraway land.

Joseph was now a slave. Even still, he did not stop believing. Joseph was sure that God would save him.

And that's just what God did. Joseph was made servant to a rich man, a man who knew a good worker when he saw one. He soon put Joseph in charge of his whole estate. Joseph had always believed that staying true to God no matter what is the best thing to do.

49

A COLORFUL COAT

Color Joseph's coat of many colors. You can also draw a pattern on it.

Decipher a Bible verse from Joseph's story using the code below.

✿ = A	✢ = K	▼ = U
■ = B	⊖ = L	◇ = V
✦ = C	▫ = M	⊘ = W
✳ = D	✱ = N	? = X
ℰ = E	● = O	✻ = Y
⊙ = F	❄ = P	△ = Z
▲ = G	◆ = Q	
❋ = H	✷ = R	
○ = I	✕ = S	
ℐ = J	▫ = T	

When Joseph came to his brothers, they pulled off his fancy coat.

Genesis 37:23 CEV

SOLD BY HIS BROTHERS

Use the clues to solve the crossword puzzle about Joseph's story.

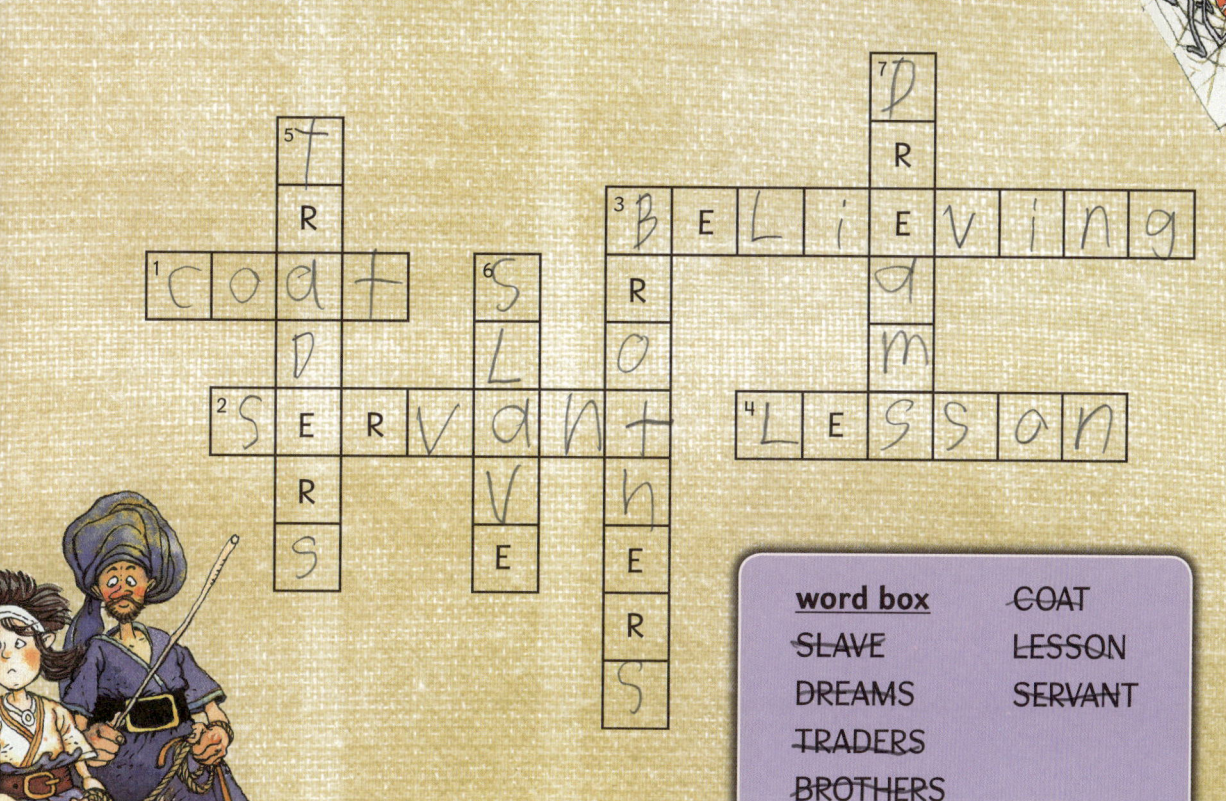

word box
- ~~SLAVE~~
- ~~DREAMS~~
- ~~TRADERS~~
- ~~BROTHERS~~
- ~~BELIEVING~~
- ~~COAT~~
- ~~LESSON~~
- ~~SERVANT~~

across
1. Joseph received a colorful _coat_ as a gift from his father.
2. After Joseph was sold, he became a _servant_ for a rich man.
3. Joseph didn't stop _believing_ in God.
4. Joseph's brothers wanted to teach him a _lesson_.

down
5. Joseph was sold to _traders_.
6. The traders treated him as a _slave_.
3. Joseph's _brothers_ were very jealous of him.
7. Joseph had a lot of _dreams_ at night.

The Faith of Joseph

Genesis 39:1—47:12

Things had just started going well for Joseph. But someone got jealous. They told a lie, and Joseph was thrown in jail. Yet like before, Joseph knew God would save him. So he did not sit in a corner, sad and glum. Instead, Joseph helped the other prisoners.

One day, the pharaoh, Egypt's king, had a dream. No one knew what it meant. Just then, the pharaoh's cupbearer spoke up. He had met a man in the jail who knew about dreams.

Joseph was brought out. "Your dream means that a famine is coming," said Joseph bravely, "so you must start saving food." The pharaoh was so grateful that he put his ring on Joseph's finger. He dressed Joseph like a king. Then he made Joseph second-in-command over all the land. Surely God was with Joseph, the king realized.

That would have been a fine ending. Yet with God, there is always more good to come. One day, Joseph's brothers came looking for food. Would the mighty ruler spare them a little corn? It had been so long, they didn't recognize Joseph.

Joseph was overjoyed to see his family. "It's me, Joseph!" he cried. Joseph forgave his brothers for selling him. Then they all went to live with Joseph in the land of plenty.

JOSEPH OUT OF PRISON

Which path did Joseph take from the prison to go see the pharaoh?

Look at Joseph carefully. Which shadow is his?

1   2   3   4

JOSEPH'S FAMILY

Write the next letter that comes in each pattern below and find out the name of Joseph's younger brother.

H - I - B - H - I - B - H - I - B - H - I -   (B)

R - R - T - E - R - R - T - E - R - R - T -   (E)

O - T - O - T - N - O - T - O - T -   (N)

A - I - R - U - J - A - I - R - U -   (J)

M - S - R - R - A - M - S - R - R -   (A)

P - E - P - M - P - E - P -   (M)

D - G - U - I - I - D - G - U - I -   (I)

Z - K - L - N - Z - K - L - N - Z - K - L -   (N)

The name is: Benjamin.

The Baby in a Basket
Exodus 1:8—2:10

A new king was in charge in Egypt, a pharaoh so awful that no one but his own family was safe.

Miriam had a new baby brother. She wanted to help keep him safe, so Miriam did just what her mother told her to do. After her mother put the baby into a basket and floated it at the edge of the river, Miriam watched from the reeds nearby to see what would happen.

The plan could not have worked out better! The royal princess came along to take her bath. Just then, her eye caught sight of something

56

strange. "Look!" she cried out to her servants. "It's a baby in a basket." The Egyptian princess scooped the baby into her arms. "I think I will adopt him," said the princess.

> The pharaoh's daughter named her adopted son Moses, which means "drawn out." "Because I drew him out of the water," she said.

A MEAN PHARAOH

The new pharaoh was afraid of the Hebrews, so he made them slaves. The Hebrews worked to build everything. Look at the picture below. Can you find:
1. 13 men working for pharaoh
2. 11 baskets

DID YOU KNOW?

The new pharaoh was one who didn't know Joseph. He looked around at all the Israelites and worried that they were becoming too mighty, and there were too many of them! He worked them really hard. That didn't help. He made them slaves. That didn't help. Finally, he ordered that their baby boys be killed. Moses was one of them. Moses's mother hid him for three months before she put him in a basket. God protected Moses.

BABY MOSES

Find the 12 hidden words taken from the story of baby Moses. They can be found up, down, across, backward, and diagonally.

```
P R T B H J R T M E R E V I R I Y R T
G R A S S G B A O L S A Y P P E D E S
R N I I L R A E T I L N A T C E K S M
S T R N T S B R H N L L K N T S U T A
I G C M C I Y C E G A Y I I A O I A I
G J N F R E J N R C N R B B N R B I R
N W M O S E S E E P G W S F G S F I
U T N W P U T S W E P L A N I X S I M
```

WORD BOX

baby	king	mother	prince
basket	Miriam	palace	princess
grass	Moses	plan	river

Which one of the babies in the basket is different? Circle it.

2   3   4

59

The Burning Bush
Exodus 2:11–3:22

Moses was a prince, but enough was enough. The pharaoh was simply too cruel for Moses to stick around. So he ran away. Moses found a new family, and life was finally starting to feel normal to him.

That's when it happened. A bush exploded into fire right in front of him. Moses had only taken the sheep to graze when, there in the wilderness, God suddenly was with him.

Moses felt afraid. What was it God wanted? "Return to Egypt," said God's voice out of the bush. God had a message for Moses to take to the pharaoh.

Moses did not feel brave. And he was awful at making speeches. But God promised to give Moses all that he needed if he obeyed. Moses was going to save God's people, the slaves of a wicked king.

"Go where I send you," said God, "and I will tell you what to say."

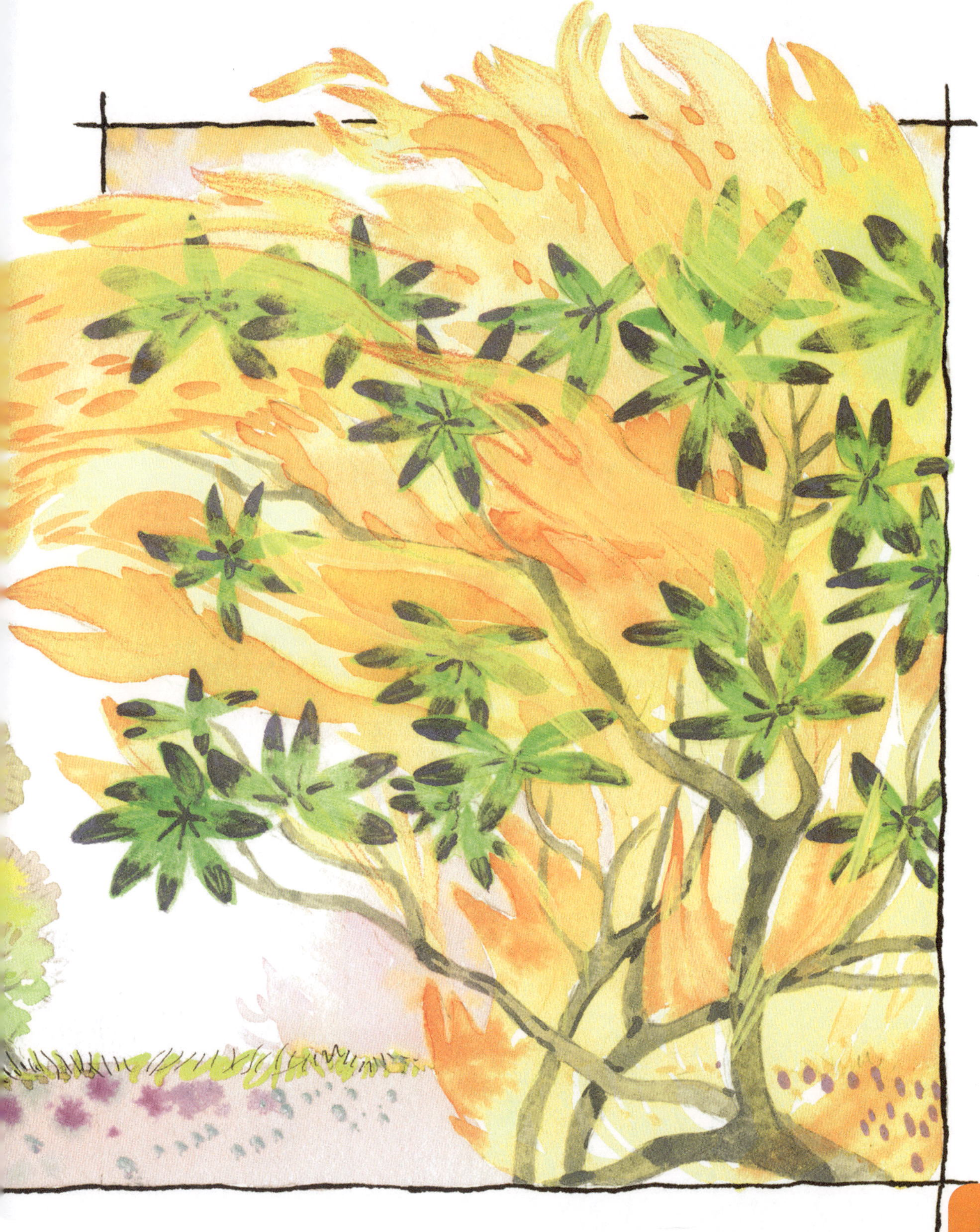

RUNNING AWAY

Find out more about what happened to Moses after he ran away. Change each bold letter to the next letter in the alphabet.

Moses ran to hide in a region called **LHCHZM**. There he married a woman named

....

Zipporah and became a **RGDOGDQC**, and

....

took care of many **ZMHLZKR**.

....

DID YOU KNOW?
Moses stuttered and stammered. That is why, when God told him to free the Israelites from slavery, he was afraid. But God had a plan.

62

MOSES'S CALLING

Find the 10 differences between the two pictures.

Find the names of four members of Moses's family: Miriam, Aaron, Jethro, and Zipporah. Cross out each name, one letter at a time, without lifting your pen until the name is complete. You can go up, down, left, or right, but each letter can only be used once.

→ | M | I | A | M | A |
| --- | --- | --- | --- | --- |
| Z | R | I | R | A |
| I | P | P | O | N |
| A | R | O | H | R |
| H | J | E | T | O |

63

Journey Through the Sea
Exodus 7–14

Moses stood in front of the pharaoh. "Let God's people *go*," said Moses. The pharaoh just laughed. Instead of letting the slaves go, he would now work them even harder.

So God turned the water to blood. Then frogs came out of the river and covered everything. The whole land soon got lice, and clouds of flies filled up the palace. Everyone got sick. There was thunder and hail, then giant bugs. Then, every firstborn died, even among the cows. At long last, the pharaoh had had enough. "Get out of here," he told Moses. "And take those slaves and those curses with you!"

The people of God packed their things. Then they fled away with Moses to guide them. He knew where to go by the pillars of smoke and fire God put in the sky.

But there was a problem—a big problem. They had run into the sea! And even worse, it looked like the king had changed his mind because here he came with his army, chasing after them. Had God led them to the sea just to get caught . . . or *drown*?

Moses reached out his staff, and God split apart the sea. Huge walls of water rose up. A dry path lay in between. The people ran across as quickly as they could. Safe on the other side, Moses reached out again. The waves closed up, and the sea was just as it had been before. All the king's army that chased them was washed away.

65

OUT OF EGYPT

Unscramble the words taken from Moses's story.

SORGF — Frogs
POLEPE — People
SVELAS — Slaves
OKSME — Smoke
FATSF — Staff
YRAM — Army
BERLPOM — Problem
VEWAS — Waves

word box

ARMY — SLAVES
FROGS — SMOKE
PEOPLE — STAFF
PROBLEM — WAVES

across

1. God put pillars of _____ in the sky to show the way.
2. What Moses and the Hebrew people faced when they arrived at the sea.
3. Washed away the king's army.
4. The king treated Moses's people as _____.

down

5. Because the king didn't listen, _____ came out of the river.
6. Moses asked the king to let his _____ go.
7. What Moses was holding in front of the sea.
8. The king's _____ was chasing Moses and his people.

66

CROSSING THE SEA

Find the close-ups in the picture.

1
2
3
4
5

67

The Promised Land
Joshua 1, 3, 6

God told Joshua, "I will never fail you. I will never leave you. All you need to do is be strong and be very brave."

God said to Joshua, "Be strong, and be brave." It was time to leave the desert. It was time to cross the Jordan. God would be with the people in every step. Joshua got the people together. Then, across the river they went. And what a lovely sight on the other side! No more sand, but a land green and lush. This was the land God had promised . . . a land of milk and honey. A land that would be their own.

There was just one problem. Jericho was a city with high stone walls. How were they ever going to beat a city like *that*?

God told Joshua just what to do. They would not use weapons—but trumpets.

Joshua knew better than to disobey God, however silly a plan might seem. He marched the people around the city just like God had said. Around, and around, and around. After seven times, everyone gave a great shout. The priests all blew their trumpets. And in one mighty quake, Jericho toppled to the ground!

BECOMING A LEADER

Use the code below to find out what God said to Joshua when he became a leader.

A=1
B=2
C=3
D=4
E=5
F=6
G=7
H=8
I=9
J=10
K=11
L=12
M=13
N=14
O=15
P=16
Q=17
R=18
S=19
T=20
U=21
V=22
W=23
X=24
Y=25
Z=26

9 22 5   3 15 13 13 1 14 4 5 4
I'Ve Commanded

25 15 21   20 15   2 5
You To Be

19 20 18 15 14 7   1 14 4
Strong And

2 18 1 22 5
Brave.

Joshua 1:9 CEV

70

JOSHUA'S STORY

Did you read the story carefully? Write the numbers 1 through 4 to put the story in order.

4

2

1

3

Gideon Wants Proof
Judges 6-7

Gideon had a hard time believing it. Did God really choose a farmer to be a warrior? Surely there was someone better. After all, the enemy was ferocious.

So Gideon had to pray to find his faith. "If You truly want me to fight," said Gideon, "then show me a sign, God. Make this wool wet while the ground stays dry." The next morning, the wool was wet. The ground was dry.

Gideon prayed again. The enemy was *so* scary that Gideon wanted to be extra sure God would be there. He hoped God would not be mad, but . . . would God now do the exact opposite? The next morning, the ground was wet, and the wool was dry.

Gideon was still small and still poor. But he now had all he needed. He had faith in God. So Gideon stormed into battle with God by his side. One hand held a trumpet. One hand held a torch. The land was saved from its enemy by only one man, who was a farmer.

"Still too many soldiers," God said to Gideon. God wanted Gideon to have the smallest army possible. That way, everyone would know it was God who won the fight, with Gideon as His servant, and not the people's own strength.

THE SMALL ARMY

Look at the pictures carefully and find the one that is different in each row.

DID YOU KNOW?
After Gideon defeated the Midianites, he was a judge over Israel for 40 years.

THE BATTLE

Find the 10 differences between the two pictures.

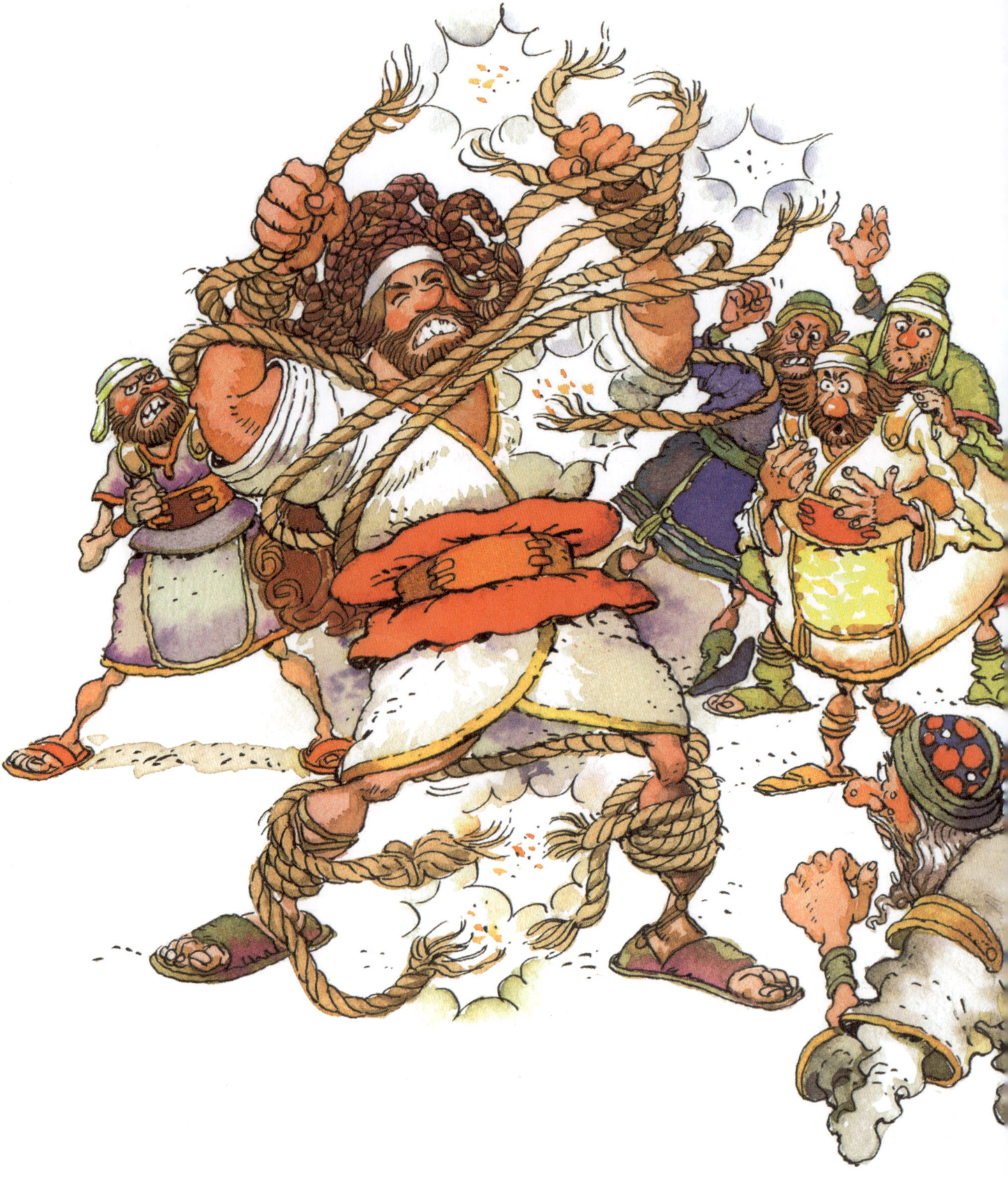

Samson the Strong
Judges 13-14, 16

He was only a kid when he once killed a lion, and with only his bare hands at that. He was stronger than strong, tougher than tough. No one could beat Samson.

His enemies would still try, of course. If only they knew his secret. *What made Samson so strong?* they wondered. *And what was it that would take his strength away?*

When a spy learned the truth, it seemed all too easy. God had ordered Samson to never cut his hair. So while Samson slept—*snip, snip*. They tied him with rope. Samson usually snapped ropes without trying. But this time, it didn't work. Samson was captured. But little did anyone realize . . .

In jail, Samson's hair just grew and grew. One day, the enemy wanted some fun. Samson was brought out. They tied him to pillars. "Look at silly Samson," they laughed.

"Please God," Samson prayed, "give me strength just one last time." Samson put his hands on the pillars. He pushed with all his might. The whole building toppled, and all of his enemies went with it.

STRONGER THAN STRONG

Join the dots and find the animal Samson killed with his bare hands.

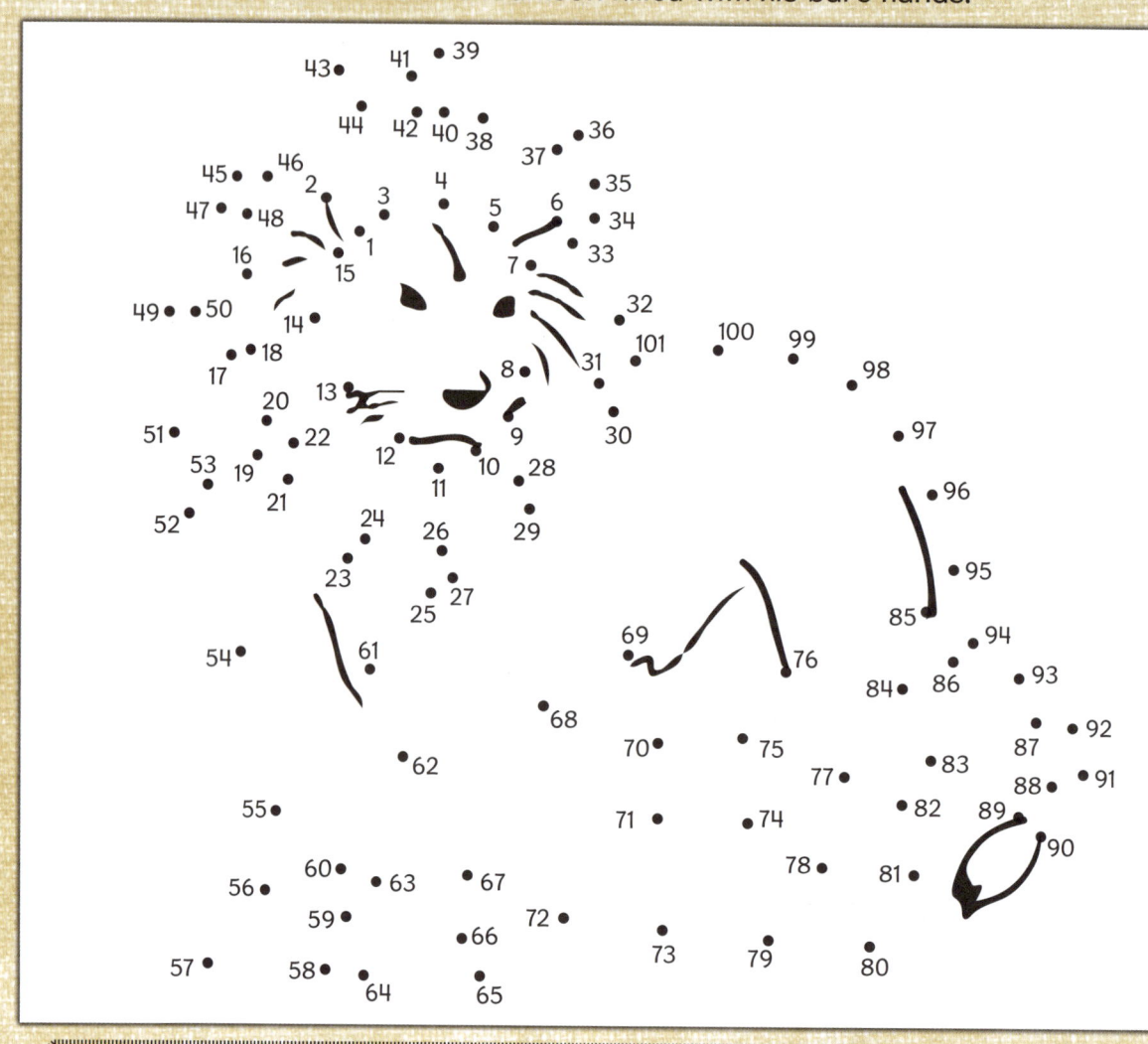

DID YOU KNOW?

Samson's mother couldn't have babies. God sent a messenger to tell her that she would have a very special son who would help deliver Israel.

Samson, whose name means "sunshine," was born during a dark period of Israel's history. At that time, the Israelites had turned from God and were under the rule of the Philistines.

SAMSON'S STRENGTH

Samson had great strengh which was given by God. Other words can be used to describe strength. In each box below, draw a line to make words with a similar meaning.

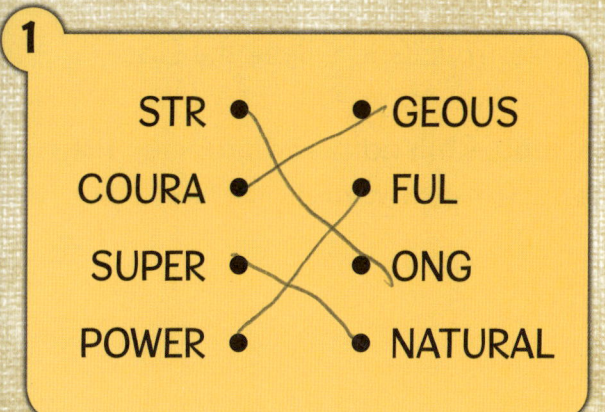

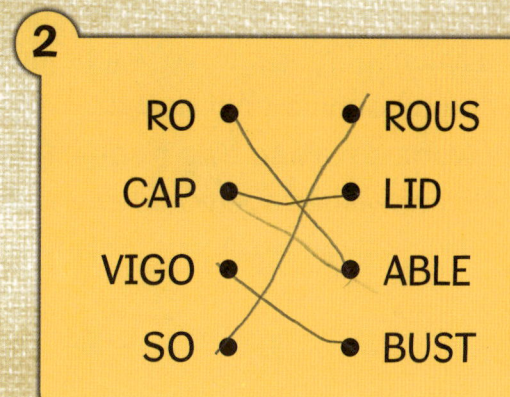

1

STR •	• GEOUS
COURA •	• FUL
SUPER •	• ONG
POWER •	• NATURAL

2

RO •	• ROUS
CAP •	• LID
VIGO •	• ABLE
SO •	• BUST

Think about your strengths—the unique gifts, talents, and abilities God has given you. Write them down.

_____

_____

_____

_____

_____

_____

_____

79

Ruth's Reward
Ruth 1–4

Ruth would not budge. Her husband had died, and her mother-in-law was letting Ruth go home. That meant Ruth could be with her old friends again. She could see her parents and get taken care of again.

Yet Ruth knew what was wrong and what was right. And she was not leaving this poor older woman to travel alone. "Where you go, I will go," Ruth said to Naomi. "Your people will be my people. Your God will be my God." What could Naomi do but agree?

Ruth worked hard to help Naomi. All day long, Ruth gathered grain for their food. Naomi wished she could pay Ruth back for all her kindness.

Naomi had an idea. Did she not have a relative named Boaz with plenty to share? Ruth had already met him. It was his field where Ruth found her grain. And what better gift for Ruth than a new chance at love.

Ruth paid a visit to Boaz. She did just as Naomi had told her. And now, Boaz had a question for Ruth . . . would she be his wife? Soon they were married, and Naomi became a grandma at last.

"I know the plans I have for you," says God. "They are plans for good and not for hurt. They are plans to give you a future and a hope. Then at last you will come to Me. You will pray, and I will listen. You will find Me when you search with all your heart."

TRAVELING HOME

Ruth and Naomi went to Bethlehem. Which path did they take?

DID YOU KNOW?
Ruth is King David's great-grandmother, and she is also the ancestor of Joseph, husband of Mary and father to Jesus.

82

LOYALTY

Decipher an important verse from Ruth's story using the code below.

A=1
B=2
C=3
D=4
E=5
F=6
G=7
H=8
I=9
J=10
K=11
L=12
M=13
N=14
O=15
P=16
Q=17
R=18
S=19
T=20
U=21
V=22
W=23
X=24
Y=25
Z=26

25 15 21 18   16 5 15 16 12 5
Y O U R   P E O P L E

23 9 12 12   2 5   13 25
W I L L   B E   M Y

16 5 15 16 12 5,   25 15 21 18
P E O P L E   Y O U R

7 15 4   23 9 12 12   2 5
G O D   W I L L   B E

13 25   7 15 4.
M Y   G O D.

Ruth 1:16 CEV

83

The Shepherd Boy
1 Samuel 16; Psalm 71

Jesse was thrilled to have the prophet Samuel in his very own home! And even more thrilled that Samuel brought wonderful news. God had chosen one of Jesse's own sons . . . to be *king!*

Jesse lined up his big, strong sons. Samuel looked over each one blankly. And now Jesse was getting worried; maybe Samuel had come to the wrong house after all. Samuel said at last, "Are these *all* your sons?"

Jesse paused. Samuel could not mean—"Well, no," said Jesse. "There's the youngest, who is out watching the sheep. But David is only a *boy!*"

Samuel seemed interested, so Jesse called David inside. As soon as

Samuel set eyes on him, his face beamed. "*That's* the one!" said Samuel. God had picked the smallest to be a king. Because to God, it's the size of the heart that matters most. Right then and there, Samuel anointed David . . . their future king.

"I will praise You with the harp," David sang. "I will sing praise to You with the lyre."

WATCHING THE SHEEP

What did David fight to protect the sheep? Color the areas with dots to find out.

Can you find which shadow matches the shape you colored?

1

2

3

4

PLAYING THE HARP

David liked to play the harp and sing. Find 12 other names of musical instruments below. They can be found up, down, across, backward, and diagonally.

```
P S T B T E N I R A L C V G R I Y R U
G A A F S G B A O L S A T R U M P E T
R X Y L O P H O N E L N A T C I K S M
S O R U T S B R H N L L P N T S T T A
I P C T C I A C C O R D I O N O I A D
G H N E R E J N R E N R A B N R B I R
N O M O S E S E E L G N S F G S F U
U N N W P V I O L I N L O A I X S I M
N E M H A R M O N I C A O S F O U Q I
```

WORD BOX

accordion	drum	harmonica	trumpet
cello	flute	piano	violin
clarinet	guitar	saxophone	xylophone

87

David and Goliath
1 Samuel 17; Psalm 148

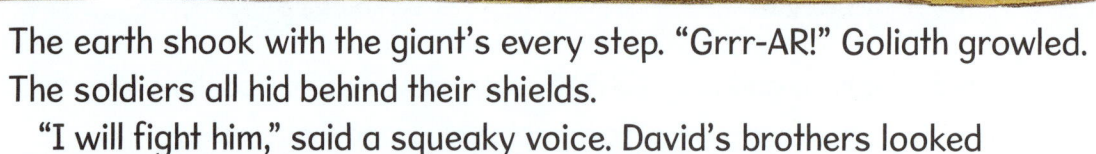

The earth shook with the giant's every step. "Grrr-AR!" Goliath growled. The soldiers all hid behind their shields.

"I will fight him," said a squeaky voice. David's brothers looked up from their hiding places. Was their younger brother trying to get himself *killed*? He was supposed to bring them lunch, then scurry home again.

David was not backing down. *What could it hurt?* thought the army leader. They tried to dress David in armor, but nothing would fit a boy. So David said no thanks. He would beat the giant with only his slingshot—and God.

Whoosh. David whirled his sling round and round. Goliath stepped forward, swinging a giant-sized sword.

"You come with a sword," yelled David, "but I come in the name of God!" Then David let loose. His rock went zooming through the air. *Crack!*—the mighty giant toppled. And so the battle was won by just a boy.

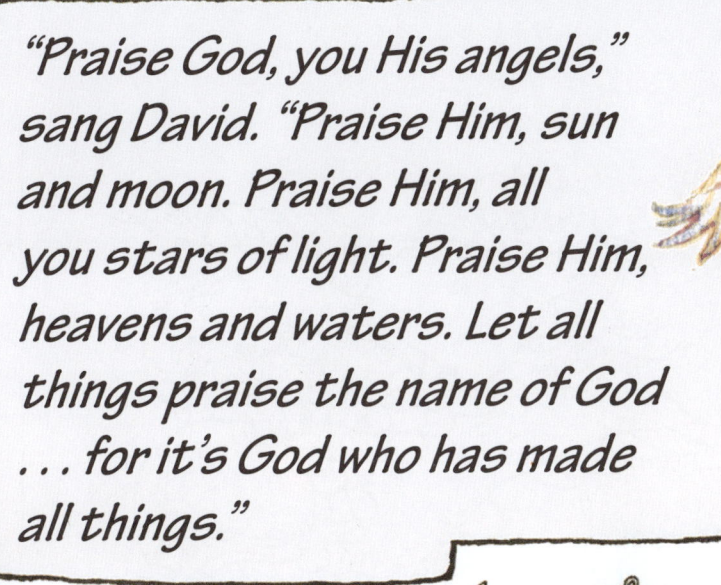

"Praise God, you His angels," sang David. "Praise Him, sun and moon. Praise Him, all you stars of light. Praise Him, heavens and waters. Let all things praise the name of God . . . for it's God who has made all things."

HIT BY A ROCK

Color Goliath being hit by the rock.

A GIANT AND A BOY

Find the 10 differences between the two pictures.

The Wisest King
1 Kings 3; Proverbs 2

King David had been loved by all. So when he died, the sadness seemed like it would never ever end.

Yet God is full of surprises. And next in line was the most famous king of all time: King Solomon the wise, David's very own son.

It had all come about in a dream when Solomon was just a young man. God had given him one wish. Instead of riches or fame, Solomon asked to be wise. God was so pleased that He gave Solomon a bonus. Not only would Solomon be wise, but he would have riches and fame as well.

It did not take long at all for his people to understand that this was a mighty king indeed. Building a house for God? Solomon was the one to make it happen. Judging right and wrong? Solomon found a way.

One day, two mothers came to him. "This is my baby," said one. "No, it's mine," said the other. Yet Solomon had a plan. How about if they shared the baby?

One of the women cried out, "Surely the child would be better with only one mother. Let her take the baby."

That woman had thought about the child more than herself. Now King Solomon knew *she* was the baby's real mother.

"If you ask for understanding," said Solomon, "if you look for it like silver or hidden treasure, then you will understand the truth that comes from God. For it's God who gives all wisdom and all knowledge."

BUILDING A TEMPLE

Can you find:
1. a dog chasing a cat
2. a man carving the wall
3. a woman serving a drink
4. four hammers

SOLOMON'S WISDOM

Which shadow belongs to the man holding the baby?

1   2   3

Find out some facts about God's temple by changing all the bold letters with the letter that comes before it in the alphabet.

In the **GPVSUI** year of his reign, Solomon began

....

the **DPOTSUVDUJPO** of the Temple. **TFWFO**

....

years later it was completed, and the **BSL** of the

....

DPWFOBOU was moved to the Temple.

....

95

Elijah the Prophet
1 Kings 17

The meanest of kings was no match for a prophet. Elijah would deliver any message God told him. Even if it put him in danger so that he had to hide out. In the woods or in the desert, God was always taking care of his people.

The king was getting punished just like Elijah had warned him. There was a famine in the land. Elijah's belly rumbled. God told him to go into town.

The woman at the town gate was gathering firewood when she heard the man's voice. He wanted a bit of bread. "Sir," said the woman, "I have barely enough for me and my son!"

Elijah told the woman she would never run out if she helped him. She made him some bread, just as he asked, using up the last of her flour and oil. But the jars weren't empty! Every day there was enough to make more bread. God was taking care of Elijah and the widow and her son.

Even before Elijah met the widow, God was taking care of him. Elijah had the evil king on his tail. "Leave from here," God told him. "Go east, and hide by a brook. You will drink from this brook, and I will send ravens to feed you." Elijah obeyed. Morning and night, the ravens dropped bread and meat from their beaks for him.

ELIJAH THE PROPHET

Unscramble the words taken from the story of Elijah and use the clues to solve the crossword puzzle.

ERDAB
MAFIEN
SAVREN
ORBOK
SEGEMAS
NAWOM
THORPPE
RULFO

word box

PROPHET   FLOUR
MESSAGE   BROOK
FAMINE   RAVENS
WOMAN   BREAD

across

1. What did Elijah ask for from the woman gathering firewood?
2. The place God told Elijah to hide so he could have water.
3. Elijah was a prophet; that meant he delivered any _____ from God.

down

4. Because there was no rain, there was a great _____.
5. God sent _____ to feed Elijah.
6. A poor _____ gave food to Elijah.
7. Elijah was a great _____.
8. What the poor woman used to make bread for Elijah.

98

ELIJAH AND THE RAVENS

Which way did the ravens take to bring food to Elijah?

FACTS ABOUT RAVENS

Ravens are cousins to crows but are bigger and have a larger and heavier black beak. They are unusually intelligent. Like other corvids, ravens can mimic sounds from their environment, including human speech.

Esther, Brave and Fair
Esther 2–8

Who was the fairest in all the land? When the king met Esther, the rest were history. Esther was all that a queen should be . . . she was good and beautiful and wise.

Esther was one more thing. She was a stranger in the land, a Jew. The king didn't know that when he agreed to let the Jews be killed!

Esther had a hard choice. The truth might destroy her, then and there.

Yet keeping her secret would have felt worse, much, much worse. So Esther got dressed in her finest gown. She dressed her heart in bravery.

"My queen!" said the king when he saw his love. "What is your wish?"

Was there anything she wanted? Esther took a deep breath. There was just one thing she wanted, Esther told the king. Would the king let Esther and her people *live*?

The king was furious that anyone would *dare* want to kill his wonderful bride! The plan had worked. Brave Queen Esther had saved her people. The king sent out a new order to stop the Jews, God's people, from being killed.

In every state and in every city, everywhere the new order came, and Esther's people had joy and gladness, a feast, and a mighty good day!

ESTHER THE QUEEN

How many overlapping crowns can you find here?

DID YOU KNOW?
Esther means "star." Esther's parents died when she was a young girl, and she was raised by her uncle.

ESTHER'S UNCLE

Write the next letter that comes in the pattern and find out the name of Esther's uncle.

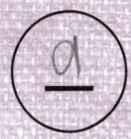

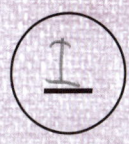

Y - U - M - Y - U - M - Y - U - M - Y - U - (M)

A - A - L - O - A - A - L - O - A - A - L - (O)

W - T - W - T - R - W - T - W - T - (R)

E - I - M - U - D - E - I - M - U - (D)

F - F - R - E - F - F - R - E - F - F - R - (E)

A - C - P - I - A - C - P - I - A - (C)

D - G - U - O - A - D - G - U - O - (A)

Q - U - L - I - Q - U - L - I - Q - U - L - (I)

His name is: M o r d e c a i .

The Lions' Den
Daniel 2:20-23; 6

How had God's servant ended up among lions? He had done everything right, after all. Daniel had obeyed God, through and through. He had served the king of the land with honor and truth.

It was a case as old as time. Daniel had done so well that others got jealous. Some rulers thought, *Why should Daniel get power?* The jealous ones tricked the king into getting rid of Daniel.

Daniel's enemies had not counted on how mighty God really was. In the darkness of the pit, Daniel prayed. Daniel believed that God would save him as He always had before.

"I give thanks to God in heaven," prayed Daniel, "to Him who uncovers things kept deep and secret. God knows all things that lie out in the darkness. And with God is where there is light."

The king was sick with worry. It was morning, and he ran to the pit of lions. Had Daniel's God been able to save him even from ferocious lions?

"I'm okay!" Daniel called up. "God has saved me," he said, to the king's relief. God had sent an angel to shut the lions' mouths.

DANIEL'S STORY

Did you read the story carefully? Write 1 through 4 to put the story in order.

DID YOU KNOW?
When the Babylonians conquered Israel, they took many young men into captivity in Babylon. One of them was Daniel. When Daniel was thrown into the lions' den, he was in his 80s.

OUT OF THE LIONS' DEN

Find the 10 differences between the two pictures.

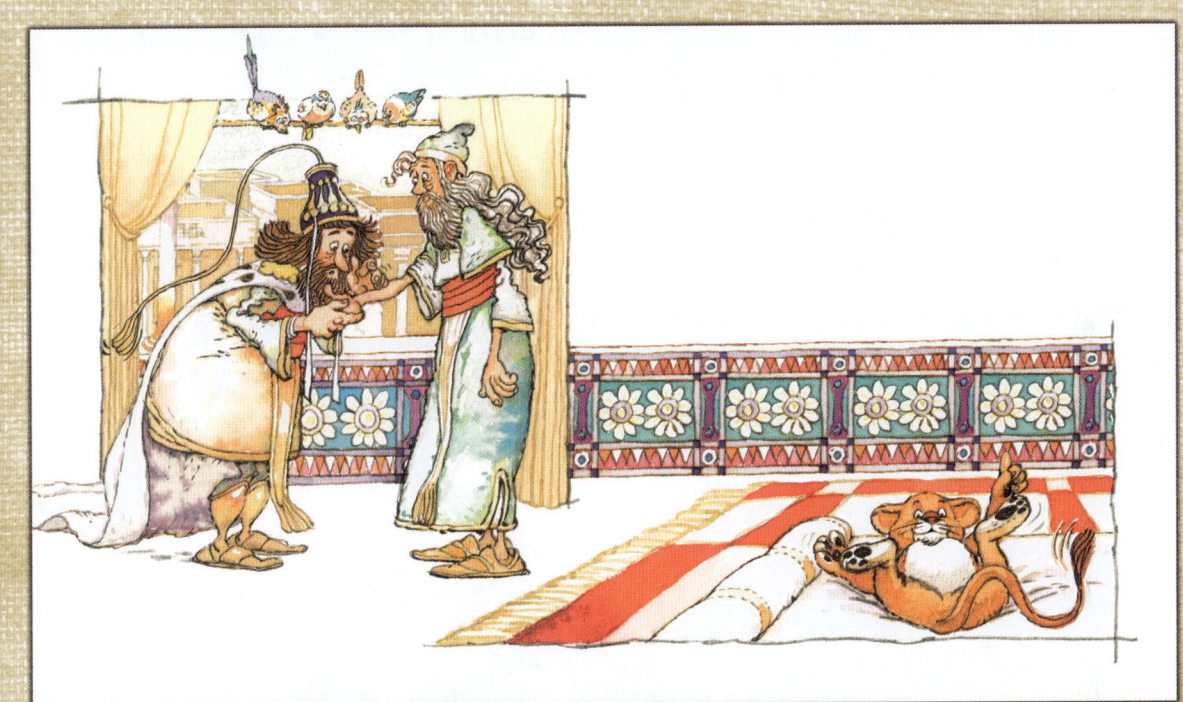

Jonah and the Whale
Jonah 1–3

Go and tell a city that God was angry? "No thank you," said Jonah. God's plan did not sound like much fun at all.

So Jonah ran away. He got on a ship sailing for a distant land. Who could find him now? Jonah thought he was free and clear.

Jonah was dead wrong. God knew exactly where Jonah was the whole time. And when that ship started shaking, Jonah knew why.

"This storm will swallow us alive!" cried one sailor.

It was time for Jonah to tell the truth—that God sent the storm because he had not obeyed. "Pick me up and throw me overboard," Jonah said, "and the sea will be calm."

Jonah bobbed in the sea, afraid and alone. But God is forgiving. And God had a plan. A giant fish swallowed Jonah up in one big *gulp!*

Inside the fish, Jonah had plenty of time to pray. He called out to God for help. He told God he was ready to obey. And with that—*splat!* The fish spit Jonah out onto land. Jonah went to Nineveh, the city that had gone bad. And Nineveh believed Jonah's message. The whole city was saved, and God used Jonah to do it.

"When deep waters surrounded me, and I was wrapped in seaweed," Jonah prayed, "You, my God, came and saved me. When I was dying, You heard my prayer."

SEA CREATURES

Which sea creature below is not a fish? Circle it.

Color the whale. Find and color 2 seahorses, 5 spotted fish, and 5 striped fish. Draw more fish.

JONAH'S STORY

Find the 12 hidden words taken from the story of Jonah. They can be found up, down, across, backward, and diagonally.

```
F U H R E Y A R P X G P
H O S R D F L E R S R U
E M R U S W A L L O W A
H J R G H T M L O Y H O
A G S A I L O R Y D A S
F R N E P V L R T T L Z
I N T R O N I D M U E S
S I H G R G B N D I A O
H N J M E S S A G E I R
Q E W F I E P G W S F R
P V T T W E V O O S I Y
E E M Q D W A N G R Y R
L H O K P M E E H B O T
```

WORD BOX

angry	Nineveh	sorry
fish	prayer	storm
forgiving	sailor	swallow
message	ship	whale

111

The New Testament

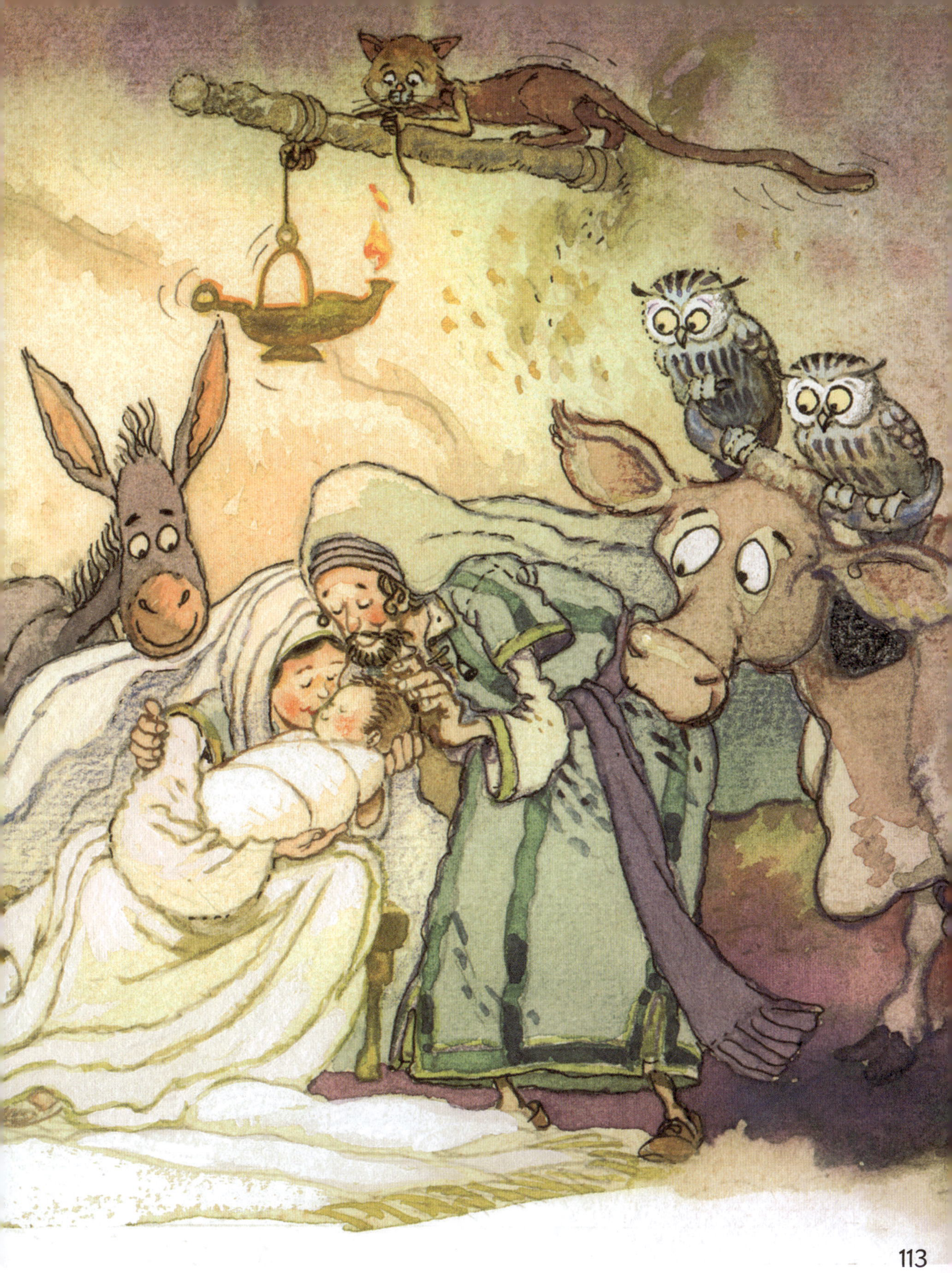

Mary and Joseph
Matthew 1:18-25; Luke 1:26-38; 2:1-7

Mary had just gotten some wonderful news. An angel named Gabriel had paid her a visit. "You are going to have a baby," Gabriel told her. "He will be the Son of God." Mary felt like the luckiest person on earth.

There was only one problem. Mary was supposed to marry a man named Joseph. How was Joseph going to feel about Mary giving birth to God's Son?

Well, God took care of that. He sent an angel to Joseph, as well. The angel explained to Joseph that a gift was on its way. "You shall call the baby Jesus," said the angel. Joseph listened carefully. When the time came, Joseph would take good care of Mary and of Jesus.

The time was very near. Mary rode on a donkey as Joseph led the way. All of the inns were full. They would stay the night in a stable instead.

THE ANGELS' VISITS

Which shadow belongs to the angel?

1   2   3

STORY QUIZ
Did you read the story carefully? Try to answer the following questions:

1. What was the name of the angel who visited Mary?

2. What news did he bring to Mary?

3. Who else had a visit from an angel? Why?

DID YOU KNOW?
Angel Gabriel also appeared to the prophet Daniel hundreds of years before and explained a vision to Daniel.

MARY AND JOSEPH

When they arrived in Bethlehem, Joseph and Mary found a stable to spend the night. Find where the stars fit into the picture and write that number there.

1   2   3   4   5

117

A King Is Born
Luke 2:1-20

On a clear and perfect night, Jesus Christ was born. This tiny baby was God's own Son. The Savior of the world had come to earth.

Mary and Joseph wrapped Jesus in cloths. They laid Him in a manger on a soft bed of hay.

Nearby, shepherds were watching their sheep, and an angel appeared to them. "Good news!" said the angel. "A Savior has been born—Christ the Lord! You'll find Him lying in a manger." The shepherds hurried off to see the baby king.

The shepherds praised God for everything they saw and heard.

THE NATIVITY STORY

Decipher the words of praise spoken by the angels of heaven to the shepherds who were watching their flocks. Use the code below.

A=1
B=2
C=3
D=4
E=5
F=6
G=7
H=8
I=9
J=10
K=11
L=12
M=13
N=14
O=15
P=16
Q=17
R=18
S=19
T=20
U=21
V=22
W=23
X=24
Y=25
Z=26

16 18 1 9 19 5   7 15 4   9 14
○ ○ ○ ○ ○ ○   ○ ○ ○   ○ ○

8 5 1 22 5 14   16 5 1 3 5
○ ○ ○ ○ ○ ○ !   ○ ○ ○ ○ ○

15 14   5   1 18 20 8   20 15
○ ○   ○   ○ ○ ○ ○   ○ ○

5 22 5 18 25 15 14 5   23 8 15
○ ○ ○ ○ ○ ○ ○ ○   ○ ○ ○

16 12 5 1 19 5 19   7 15 4
○ ○ ○ ○ ○ ○ ○   ○ ○ ○ .

Luke 2:14 CEV

120

JESUS IS BORN

Find 10 differences in the two pictures.

The prophet had written: "Bethlehem, in Judah, out of you will come a king who will shepherd God's people Israel."

Three Wise Men
Matthew 2:1-12

In a land far away, wise men saw a star. They knew just what the star meant. The Christ had been born, the king of the Jews.

They followed the star to where Jesus lay. When they saw Him, the wise men knelt down with joy. They gave Him precious gifts that they carried from the east . . . frankincense, gold, and sweet-smelling myrrh.

STAR OF BETHLEHEM

The wise men were guided by the bright star to find the king of the Jews. Which way did they take?

THE WISE MEN'S GIFTS

Each gift the wise men brought to Jesus was very precious. Each of these gifts was showing who Jesus is and what His mission was. Find the right description for the right picture.

1 • MYRRH

2 • GOLD

3 • FRANKINCENSE

A • was often a gift given to a king. It represents the fact that Jesus was royal and would rule the kingdom of God.

B • is an aromatic resin that was used as incense in temples and churches. It was reserved for the worship of God. This gift represents the fact that Jesus was indeed divine.

C • is an aromatic resin that was used for incense, perfume, and medicine. Its major use was for burials. It is said to represent that Jesus came into the world to die for our sins.

DID YOU KNOW?

The wise men are also called magi. They were wise men from the east. The Bible does not say there were *three* wise men. Tradition says that because of the three gifts brought to Jesus.

Fishers of Men
Matthew 4:18-22; 13:47-50; Luke 2:41-52; 4:1-13; 5:1-11

Jesus grew up strong and good and wise. He was only twelve when He started teaching the teachers at the temple. Jesus knew more about the kingdom of God than anyone else around. And He should have, of course, because Jesus was God's own Son.

When Jesus was all grown up, it was time to leave home. It was time to do God's work. Jesus went into the wilderness to pray for forty days. Afterward, Jesus was strong, and He was ready.

Jesus needed helpers. He saw two men in a fishing boat. "Follow me," said Jesus, "and I will make you fishers of men." One by one, Jesus picked His friends who wanted to serve God and who were ready to share God's love. They would be called disciples. And wherever Jesus went, His disciples would follow.

Jesus said, "The kingdom of God is like a net. It gathers all kinds of fish. The bad fish are thrown out; the good fish are saved. Just like this, the good, the ones who believe in me, will join me in heaven."

THE 12 DISCIPLES OF JESUS

Using the word box below, label the picture with the names of the 12 disciples.

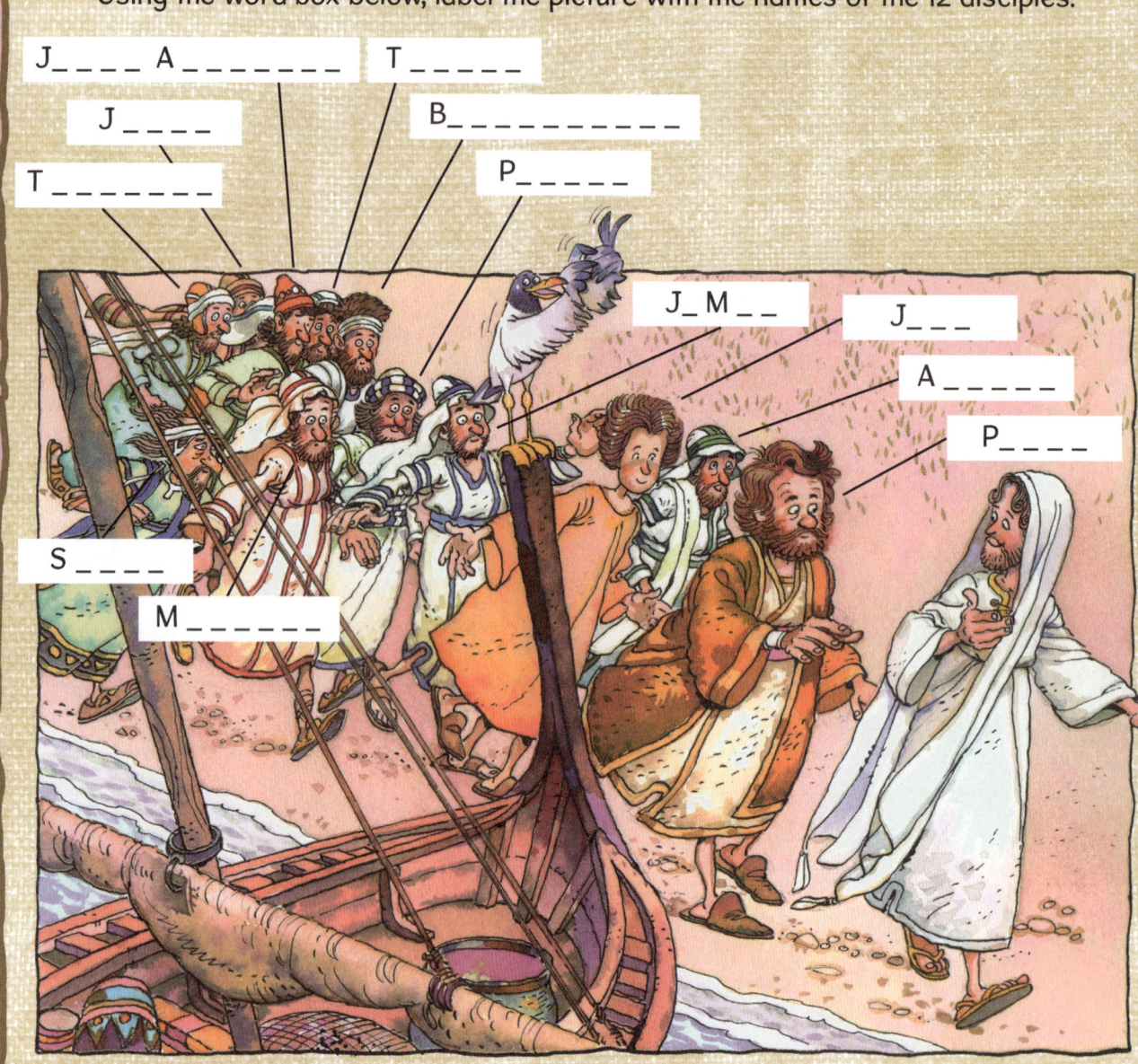

J_ _ _ _ A_ _ _ _ _ _ _ _
J_ _ _ _
T_ _ _ _ _ _ _
T_ _ _ _ _
B_ _ _ _ _ _ _ _ _ _
P_ _ _ _ _
J_M_ _
J_ _ _
A_ _ _ _ _
P_ _ _ _
S_ _ _ _
M_ _ _ _ _ _

word box

Andrew	James Alphaeus	Matthew	Simon
Bartholomew	John	Peter	Thaddeus
James	Judas	Philip	Thomas

128

FOLLOWING JESUS

Find out what Jesus said to Simon and his brother Andrew by changing the bold letters to the next letter that comes in the alphabet.

IDRTR said to them, " **BNLD** with me! I will **SDZBG** you

....

how to **AQHMF** in people instead of **EHRG**." Mark 1:17 CEV

....

Color the areas with dots to find what symbol early Christians used as a secret Christian symbol.

DID YOU KNOW?
The disciples had no extraordinary skills. They were ordinary people, but God chose them for a purpose. They left their homes, jobs, and friends to follow Jesus.

Love Your Enemy
Matthew 5; 13:24-30

GROW GOOD THINGS

Can you find 10 grasshoppers in this picture?

The Loving Father
Luke 15:11-32

Jesus told a story of a man who had two sons. The younger acted greedy and selfish. "I don't want to wait," he told his father. "I want the money you saved for me—right *now*." The father hated seeing his son upset. So, the father agreed. *Clink, clink, clink,* the coins were counted out. Then the son went skipping away, ready for some fun.

It wasn't long, not long at all. The money had not lasted like he thought it would when at first it was so heavy in his pocket. The young man was too ashamed to go home. So he took a job instead. He would shovel pig manure and maybe get to eat with the pigs.

His stomach growled. The son could not stand it a moment more. He was going to take his chances. Maybe his father would forgive him enough to let him be a servant in his house.

When the father saw his son, he ran out of the house. His beloved son was home safe and sound! He would not let him be a servant. This was his son, and he would be treated like one still. The father put him back in fine clothes and called for a feast.

"Just like this story," Jesus said, "your Father in heaven forgives. God is glad when His precious child comes home."

SKIPPING AWAY

Here are 4 pictures of the son leaving his father. Two of them are exactly the same. Which two?

1

2

3

4

DID YOU KNOW?
This story is also called the Prodigal Son. *Prodigal* means to spend a lot of money on things we don't need and to be very wasteful.

136

A FORGIVING FATHER

Decipher the words spoken by the father to his older son, who didn't forgive his younger brother. Use the code below.

A=1
B=2
C=3
D=4
E=5
F=6
G=7
H=8
I=9
J=10
K=11
L=12
M=13
N=14
O=15
P=16
Q=17
R=18
S=19
T=20
U=21
V=22
W=23
X=24
Y=25
Z=26

2 21 20 — 23 5 — 19 8 15 21 12 4

2 5 — 7 12 1 4 — 1 14 4

3 5 12 5 2 18 1 20 5 !

25 15 21 18 — 2 18 15 20 8 5 18

23 1 19 — 4 5 1 4 ,

2 21 20 — 8 5 — 9 19

14 15 23 — 1 12 9 22 5 .

Luke 15:32 CEV

Water into Wine
John 2:1-11; 15:1-2

"Thank goodness you're here," said Mary when Jesus arrived. There was a problem. "The wedding has run out of wine!" Mary cried. How embarrassing this would be for the bride and groom with so many important guests.

Mary knew that her son was just the one to save the day. "Whatever Jesus tells you," said Mary to the servants, "do it."

Jesus asked for big jars. He told them to fill each one with water. The servants took pitchers to the table. Were they really supposed to fill up wine glasses with only water? With shaky hands, the servants started to pour. Yet instead of water, the pitchers poured out wine! Jesus had done his first miracle of many.

The master of the feast cleared his throat. He declared that this was the best wine yet!

"I am the true vine," said Jesus, "and my Father is the gardener. He cuts off the branches that don't have fruit. He keeps the rest healthy to make even more fruit."

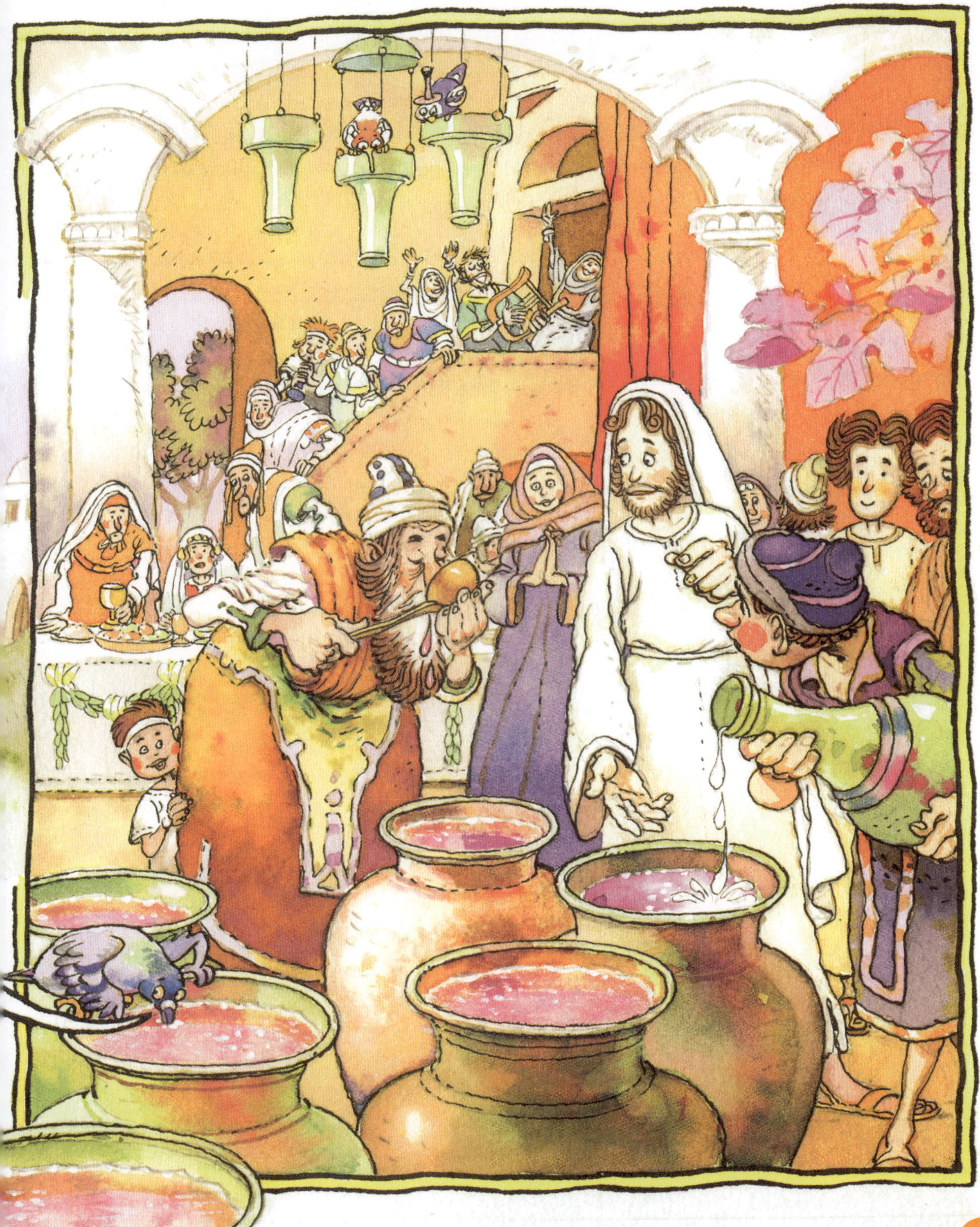

WEDDING AT CANA

The wedding was taking place in Cana, a small village in Galilee. Weddings were very important celebrations among the Jewish people. Find out where the 5 pictures go, and write the number in the circle.

THE TRUE VINE

Jesus called himself the true vine. God is the gardener, and we are the . . .

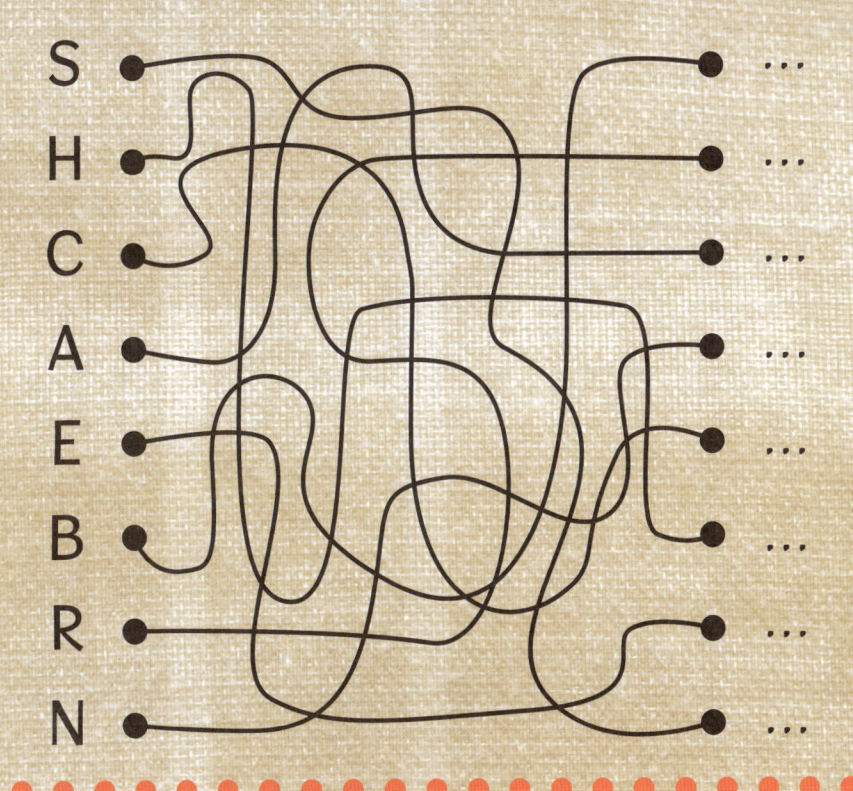

S
H
C
A
E
B
R
N

DID YOU KNOW?
How many overlapping jars can you find here? _____

Turning water into wine at the wedding in Cana was Jesus's first miracle.

The Miracles of Jesus
Matthew 8–9; Mark 2:1-12; John 21:25

It had not taken long for the news to spread. This was no ordinary man. Jesus could make people walk who couldn't walk before. He could make the blind able to see. He could make the deaf able to hear. Jesus could heal anyone!

"Lord," called a sick man, "I believe You can heal me." Right away, the man was well. When Peter's mother got a fever, Jesus healed her with just a touch. Men with diseases went leaping away with joy. One woman touched only His robe, and she was made well.

One day, Jesus was in a house of doctors and lawyers. All of a sudden, the roof opened up. A man was lowered down with ropes—putting him right in front of Jesus. The house had been so full that the sick man's friends had to let him in through the roof.

Jesus was amazed. What great friends the sick man had! Great friends with great faith. And that was all Jesus needed to see to heal the man.

Jesus did many other things too. If they were all written in books, the whole world wouldn't be big enough to hold all the books!

143

HEALING THE SICK

Jesus showed love and compassion for others when he healed people. Color Jesus healing the sick man and the people witnessing the miracle.

DID YOU KNOW?
The four gospels record 37 miracles of Jesus, but Jesus did many other things as well that were not recorded.

JESUS'S MIRACLES

Find out what Jesus said to the paralyzed man by changing the bold letters to the letters that come before them in the alphabet.

"**HFU VQ**! Pick up your **NBU** and go on **IPNF**." Mark 2:11 CEV

....

Jesus performed many miracles. Match the words to find some of Jesus's miracles.

TURNED WATER	THE SICK
DROVE OUT	TO LIFE
HEALED	THE STORM
RAISED	INTO WINE
CALMED	EVIL SPIRITS

145

The Great Storm

Mark 4:35-41

Things had gone from bad to worse. Giant waves now splashed aboard. It was time to wake up the boss. "Jesus," cried a disciple, "we are all going to *drown!*"

Jesus calmly got up. He went to the front of the boat where the storm whirled all around Him. Then He raised His hands toward the sea. "Peace!" said Jesus. "Be still." Right away, the storm obeyed. The wind died down. All was calm.

Jesus looked at His disciples. "Why were you afraid?" He asked them. The disciples just stared back . . . Jesus had power even over the wind and sea!

147

DON'T BE AFRAID

Find 10 differences between the two pictures below.

CALMING THE STORM

Unscramble the words taken from the story of Jesus calming the storm, and use the clues to solve the crossword puzzle.

LITLS
PIDISCSEL
ACEEP
WEPOR
TROMS
NDOWR
VESAW
NWID

word box

STORM   PEACE
WAVES   STILL
DISCIPLES   WIND
DROWN   POWER

across
1. Jesus raised His hands and said, "_____."
2. One of the disciples thought they were all going to _____.
3. There were giant _____ waves.
4. The _____ calmed down when Jesus commanded.
5. Jesus also told the sea to be _____.

down
1. Jesus has great _____.
2. The _____ were afraid.
6. The _____ were splashing aboard.

149

The Endless Feast
John 6:1-15

The answer was not good. "We only have what this boy gave us," said a disciple. "Just two fish and five loaves of bread." How were they ever going to feed more than five thousand people? They didn't have enough money for that. Everyone was worried.

   Everyone, that is, but Jesus. He held the food up and prayed. Then Jesus began to break the bread and fish. Into large baskets, the pieces fell. One basket was soon full, then another . . . and another! Jesus filled basket after basket without ever running out. All of the people could now eat as much as they wanted. And when no one could eat another bite, there were leftovers to save for later.

151

LOAVES AND FISH

Color the A's blue and the B's brown.
What is the picture? _____

152

FEEDING THE 5,000

Can you find and circle in the picture below:

1. three baskets
2. seven fish skeletons
3. two cats

153

154

Back from the Dead
John 11:1-44

Jesus felt His heart nearly break. He had come too late. Lazarus was already dead. Jesus went to the cave where His good friend was buried, and He cried.

Yet—He was Jesus after all. "Take away the stone," Jesus ordered. Then He looked up to heaven. Jesus prayed to God, saying, "Father, thank You for hearing Me."

What happened next was the most amazing miracle yet. "Lazarus!" called Jesus with a loud voice. "Come out of there." Lazarus stepped out of the cave just as alive as ever. His sisters ran to him, crying with joy. And all who saw this believed.

Jesus said to Martha, Lazarus's sister, "I am the one who can raise the dead and give life. Everyone who believes in Me will live. And those who believe will see the glory of God."

ON THE WAY TO LAZARUS

Mary and Martha sent for Jesus when their brother, Lazarus, got sick. Help Jesus find the way to Lazarus's home in Bethany.

DID YOU KNOW?
Lazarus and his two sisters, Mary and Martha, were friends of Jesus.

A GREAT MIRACLE

Find the 12 hidden words taken from the story of Lazarus. They may be up, down, across, backward, or diagonal.

```
G L M I R A C L E P
W A N C O P H B E E
L Z M F R I E N D V
R A E A M A A N S A
L R O I Z L V H T C
S U N T H I E E O G
D S A H E V N E N H
E A S F A E H G E S
A E B U R I E D L U
D D E S I S T E R S
```

WORD BOX

alive	dead	Lazarus
amazing	faith	miracle
buried	friend	sisters
cave	heaven	stone

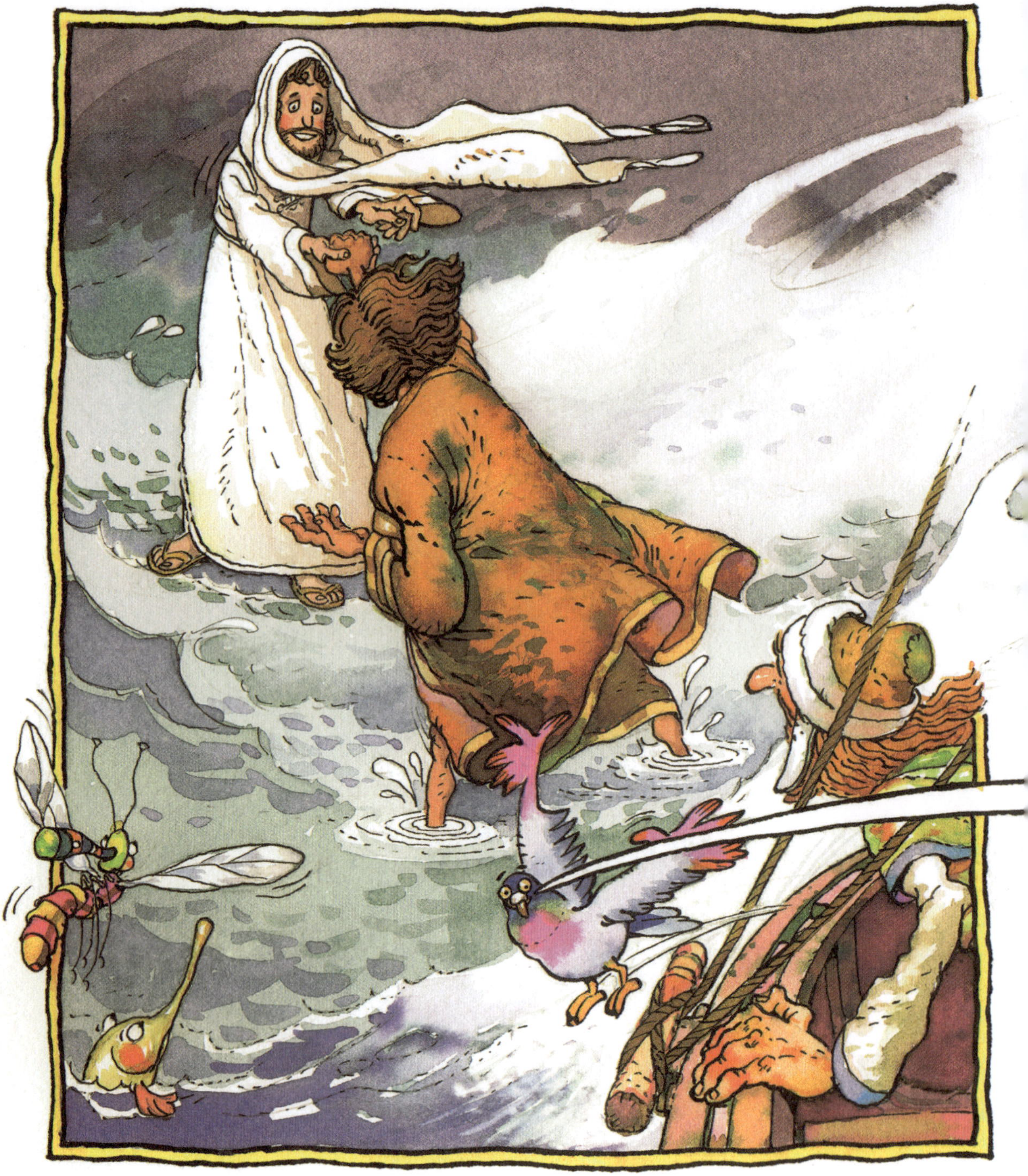

Jesus Walks on Water
Matthew 14:22-33; 17:20

The boat rocked back and forth. *If only Jesus were here*, thought the disciples. Jesus would stop the storm, and they'd be saved. But instead, the storm grew worse and worse.

Just then—what was that out on the sea? Through the darkness, the disciples saw the shape of a man. He was walking on the water . . . and coming *straight* for them. They were terrified—a *ghost!*

"Fear not," came the voice. "It's me, Jesus."

Peter wasn't so sure. "If it's really you," said Peter, "then let me walk out to You." Jesus agreed. So with shaky legs, Peter swung himself over the edge of the boat. He took one step, then another. Peter was walking on water! And in the middle of a scary storm too. Peter felt the wind tug at his hair. He looked across at the size of the waves. Then—*ker-splash*—Peter toppled into the water. "Save me!" Peter cried.

Jesus grabbed his hand. "Peter," said Jesus, "why did you not believe?"

"I tell you the truth," said Jesus. "It takes the tiniest bit of faith, the size of a mustard seed, to do something amazing. With God, nothing is impossible."

JESUS AND PETER

Find out where the pieces of the puzzle go to reconstruct the picture.

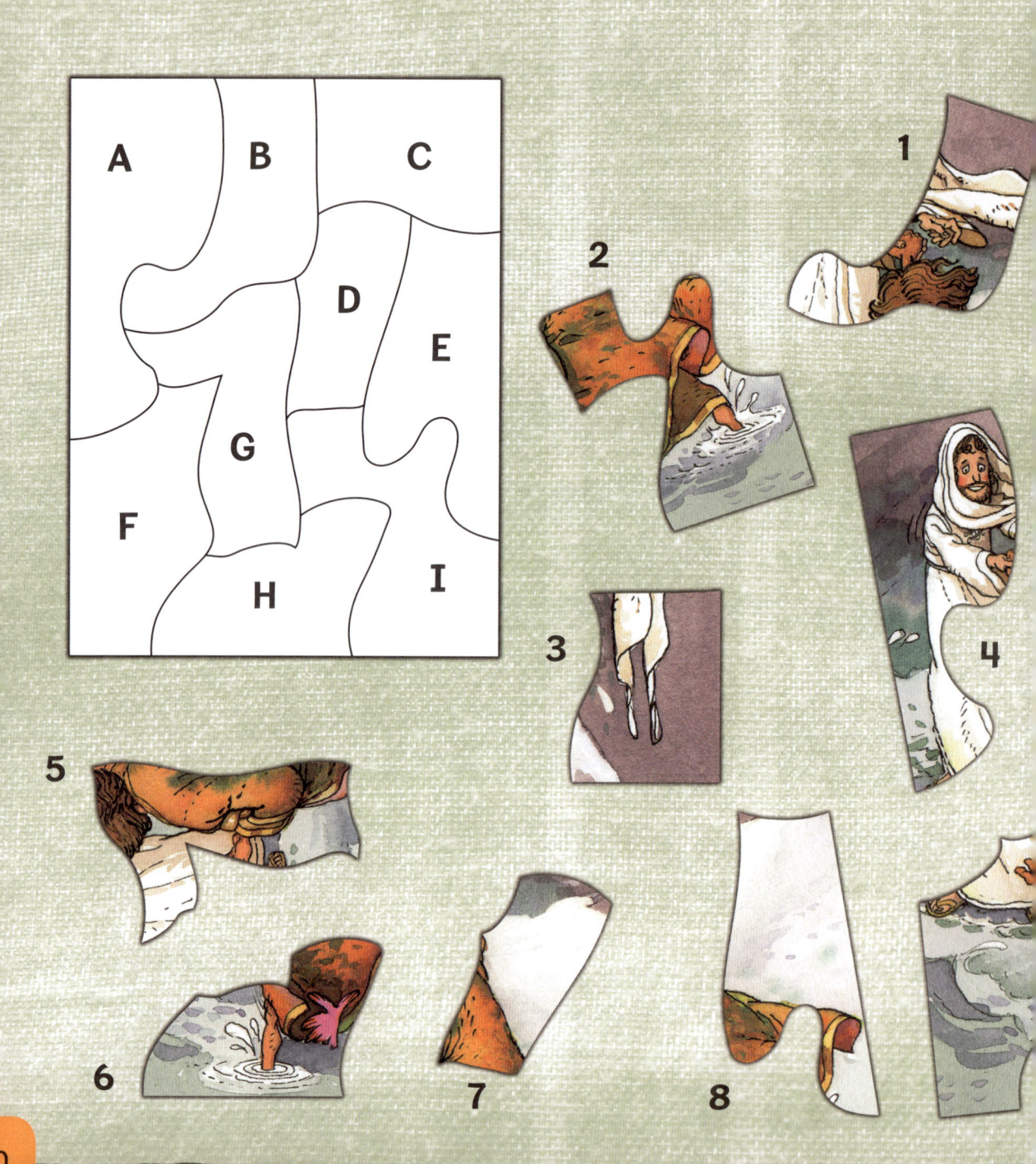

JESUS'S MIRACULOUS POWER

Use the code to decipher the Bible verse below to find out what the disciples said to Jesus.

A=1
B=2
C=3
D=4
E=5
F=6
G=7
H=8
I=9
J=10
K=11
L=12
M=13
N=14
O=15
P=16
Q=17
R=18
S=19
T=20
U=21
V=22
W=23
X=24
Y=25
Z=26

20 8 5   13 5 14   9 14

20 8 5   2 15 1 20

23 15 18 19 8 9 16 5 4

10 5 19 21 19   1 14 4   19 1 9 4,

"25 15 21   18 5 1 12 12 25   1 18 5

20 8 5   19 15 14   15 6   7 15 4."

Matthew 14:33 CEV

161

Let the Children Come
Mark 10:13-16

Everyone wanted to see Jesus. The mothers brought their little ones for Jesus to bless. The children crowded as close as they could get.

The disciples got annoyed. Jesus had important things to do! There were lessons to be taught. There were people to be healed. *Jesus did not have time to bother with kids,* thought His friends. So they tried to send all the children away.

Jesus saw what His friends were doing. And Jesus did not like it at all. "Do not send the children away," He told his friends. "Let them come to me because it is *children* who hold the keys to heaven."

"Listen to me," said Jesus. "No one may enter God's kingdom unless they come like a little child." They must not act high and mighty or think they know it all. Instead, the kingdom of God is for those whose heart is pure. It is for those who can listen. It is for those who can believe.

JESUS AND THE CHILDREN

Jesus loves children. They are very special in His eyes. Color the scene of Jesus with the children below.

"COME TO ME"

Look at these pictures carefully. Which one is different?

Jesus also taught His disciples about what is important. Find out what He said to them by changing the bold letters to the next letter in the alphabet.

"If you want to be **FQDZS**, you must be the **RDQUZMS** of

....

all the **NSGDQR**." Mark 10:43 CEV

....

165

Hosanna to the King
Matthew 21:1-11

"Hosanna," called the people. Their King had come! They waved big palm branches as Jesus passed by.

Jesus did not wear fancy robes. He did not ride a mighty stallion. Instead, Jesus wore plain robes and rode on a donkey that bumped along on the way to the city.

People had come out to see Him for miles around. This was the one who was going to save them from all troubles, they thought. They spread their clothes on the ground. They made His way fit for a king. "Hosanna," they cried. "Hosanna in the highest!"

The prophet said, "Tell the people of Jerusalem their king is coming to them, riding on a young donkey."

A TRIUMPHAL ENTRY

Can you find in this picture:
1. 29 palm branches
2. a woman playing the tambourine
3. a man on a balcony

THE KING OF KINGS

Find these 4 words taken from the story: hosanna, branches, donkey, palm. Cross out each one, one letter at a time, without lifting your pencil. You can go up, down, left or right, but the letters can be used only once.

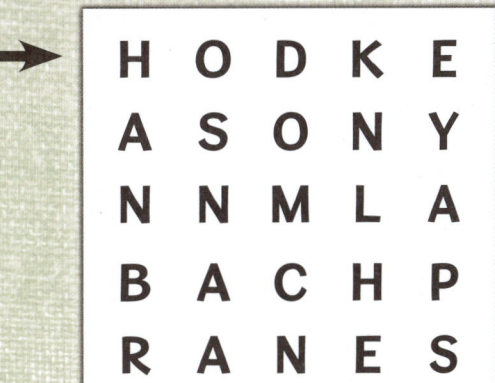

```
H O D K E
A S O N Y
N N M L A
B A C H P
R A N E S
```

Which shadow belongs to Jesus on the donkey?

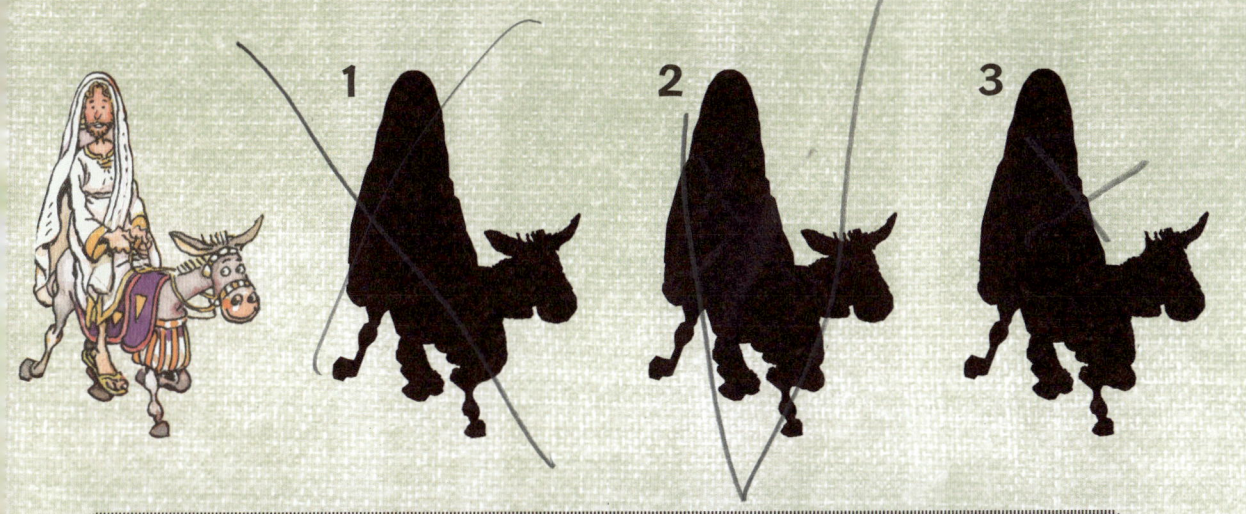

1   2   3

DID YOU KNOW?
On Palm Sunday we celebrate Jesus's triumphal entry into Jerusalem. Palm Sunday is the Sunday before Easter.

169

Jesus broke the bread and handed it to His disciples. Then He said, "This is My body, which is given for you. Eat this as a way of remembering Me!"

The Last Supper
Luke 22:14-44

Jesus had a heavy heart. It was the last time He would eat with His friends before His death and resurrection.

He passed around His cup and broke the bread. He told His friends to remember Him whenever they ate from now on. "Whoever shall be the greatest," said Jesus, "may that person act like the smallest. And whoever shall be the chief, act like a servant."

After supper, Jesus went to pray in the garden. "Dear Father," said Jesus, "may Your plan be done."

JESUS'S LAST MEAL

Draw a line to connect the zoomed-in, black-and-white pictures to where they belong in the picture. Then color them.

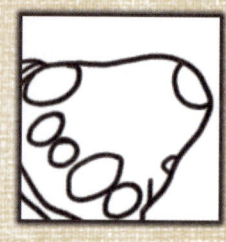

DID YOU KNOW?
At the Last Supper, Jesus showed humility by doing the task that no one wanted to do. He washed the disciples' feet. Washing someone's feet was considered a dirty job. Only servants washed people's feet.

IN THE GARDEN

Which path did Jesus take from the upper room in Jerusalem, where He had his last supper, to the garden of Gethsemane, where He went to pray.

173

Soldiers at the Garden Gate
Matthew 26:47-68; 27:11-26; John 18:1-14

Jesus and His friends were just leaving the garden when they saw a terrible sight. A group of soldiers—coming *straight* toward them.

Peter wanted to fight the soldiers. He drew his sword.

"Put that away," said Jesus. "This is God's plan." Jesus acted brave. He went with the soldiers without fighting at all.

Jesus was taken before a rowdy crowd. "Kill Him!" they yelled. But Jesus hadn't done anything wrong. "Kill Him!" the people shouted even louder.

PETER FOUGHT BACK

Trying to protect Jesus, Peter drew a sword and attacked a man named Malchus, the servant of the high priest, chopping off his ear. Jesus stopped Peter and healed the man's ear. Color the scene.

DID YOU KNOW?

The trial of Jesus took place in six stages: three before the Jewish elders and three before the Gentile authorities.

THE TRIAL OF JESUS

Following His arrest, Jesus was put on trial and sentenced to death.
Find 10 differences between the two pictures.

Peter Lies About Jesus
Luke 22:54-62

Jesus had been locked up. Now Peter stood alone, warming his hands at a fire.

"Hey, you," a voice called. Peter looked up. Nearby, a group of soldiers stood alert, their swords glittering. Were the soldiers going to take Peter away like they had taken Jesus?

The woman spoke again. "Didn't I see you with Jesus?" she asked.

"Who, me?" said Peter, ducking away.

But Peter did not get far. "That one, there!" said another. "That man is a friend of Jesus."

Peter could feel eyes burn into him from every side. The fear was starting to boil. Peter shook his head. "You have the wrong guy," he replied. A third time someone asked him if he was a follower of Jesus, and for the third time, Peter said no. Then Peter hurried off.

Just then . . . *cock-a-doodle-do!* The cry of a rooster shook Peter to his senses. Suddenly, Peter realized—he had lied. Peter had pretended not to be a friend of Jesus when it mattered the most. Peter's heart filled with sadness, more sorry than words.

Jesus had said, "I tell you, Peter, before the rooster crows today, you will lie three times, pretending that you don't know Me."

179

PETER'S DENIAL

Find the 12 hidden words taken from the story of Peter. They may be up, down, across, backward, or diagonal.

```
D U S R E I D L O S
N A R O S W O R D S
E N O F A T H E R S
I W O M A N P H O S
R E S S U S E J U E
F L T D E A T R N N
C S E C O L E F T D
F I R E P O R E A A
R A M F R N E A I S
L R E P Z E V R N E
```

WORD BOX

alone	friend	sadness
Father	Jesus	soldiers
fear	Peter	swords
fire	rooster	woman

THE ROOSTER CROWED

Which silhouette matches the picture of Peter?

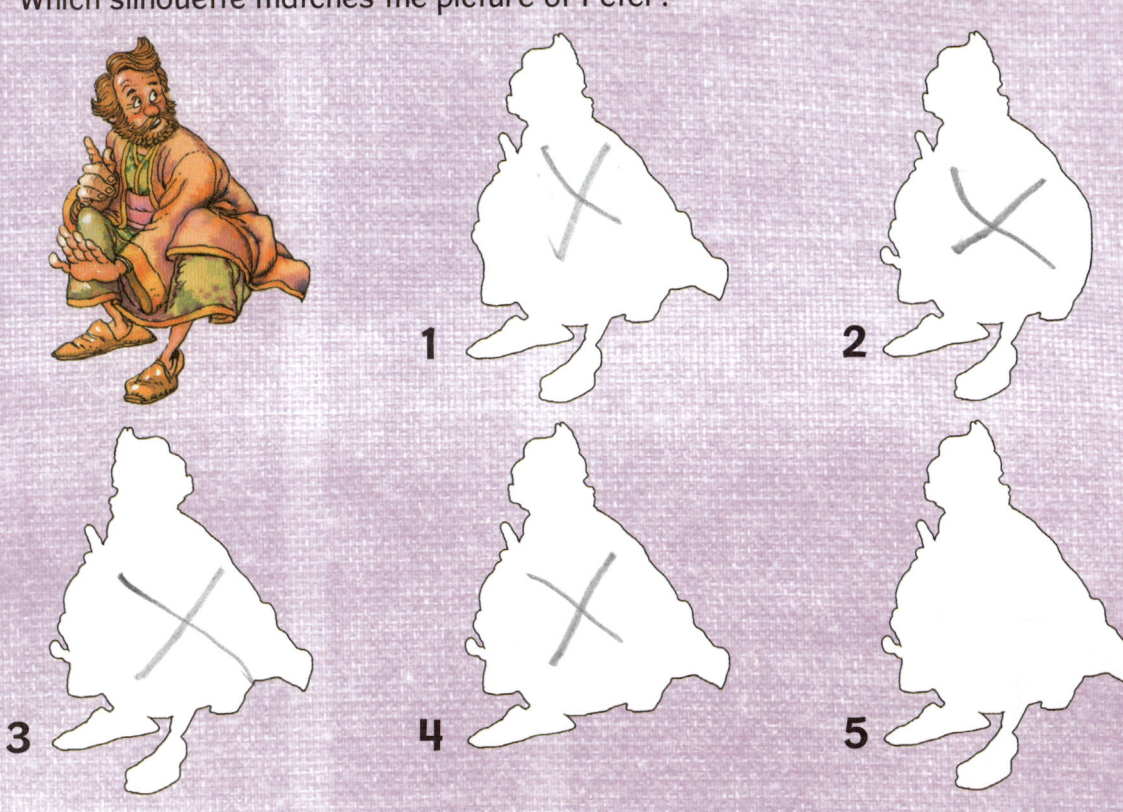

1

2

3

4

5

MEMORY GAME

Study the picture of Peter denying Jesus on page 179. Now try to answer these questions without looking back.

1. How many mice are warming up by the fire? _____

2. How many spear(s) are in the picture? _____

3. What do you see at the top right of the picture? _____

4. Who can you see in the far back in the picture? _____

181

The Cross on the Hill

Luke 23:32-46

Jesus had known He would die from the very beginning. It was the only way to save the world from sin. It was the only way He could pay our way to heaven.

They hung Jesus on a cross high on a hill. Jesus looked up to heaven. He prayed that God would forgive those who had hurt Him. Then Jesus closed His eyes, and it was done.

183

JESUS ON THE CROSS

Jesus willingly died on the cross because He loved us so much. Find these things in the picture below:

JESUS DIED FOR OUR SINS

Discover a very important Bible verse by changing the bold letters to the letter that comes before it in the alphabet.

HPE loved the **QFPQMF** of this world **TP NVDI** that

....

he gave his only **TPO**, so that **FWFSZPOF** who has

....

GBJUI in him will have **FUFSOBM** life and never

....

really **EJF.** John 3:16 CEV

....

How many overlapping crosses can you count here? ☐

185

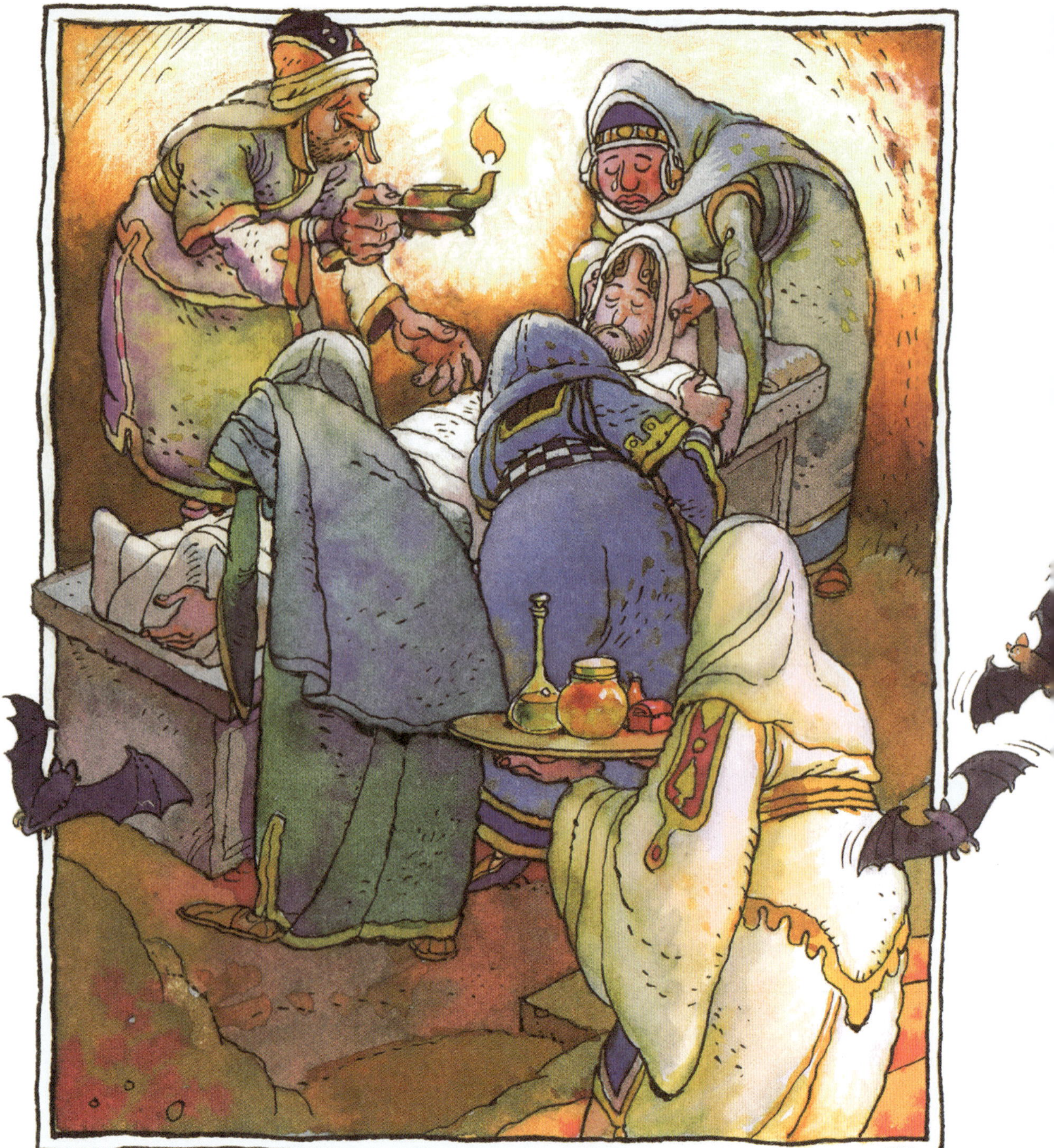

A Cave for a King
Matthew 27:57-66; John 16:16-20; 19:38-42

Jesus had died. His friends washed and perfumed Him. They wanted to give Jesus the best burial that they could. But a nice burial was going to cost money . . . a lot of money.

A rich man named Joseph came to the rescue. He wrapped Jesus up in fine, white cloth. He gave his brand-new cave for the burial. Inside the cave, Jesus was laid to rest. Each friend said goodbye. Then, a stone was rolled over the cave mouth. His friends would miss Jesus forever and always. Yet His words were tucked in their hearts to warm them with love.

Of course, not everyone was sorry Jesus had died. After a day had passed, the rulers began to worry. Didn't Jesus say that He would rise again?

The rulers were not taking chances. They made sure the cave was sealed up good and tight. Then they put soldiers outside to keep watch. No one was getting in or out.

Or so they thought. Yet God always has the final say. And nothing can be hidden that God wants brought to light.

"For a little while, you will not see Me," Jesus had told His friends. "Yet a little while more, and you will see Me again. When I'm gone, you will cry with sadness. Yet your sorrow will turn to joy. You will see Me again with a gladness that no one can take away."

JESUS'S FRIENDS

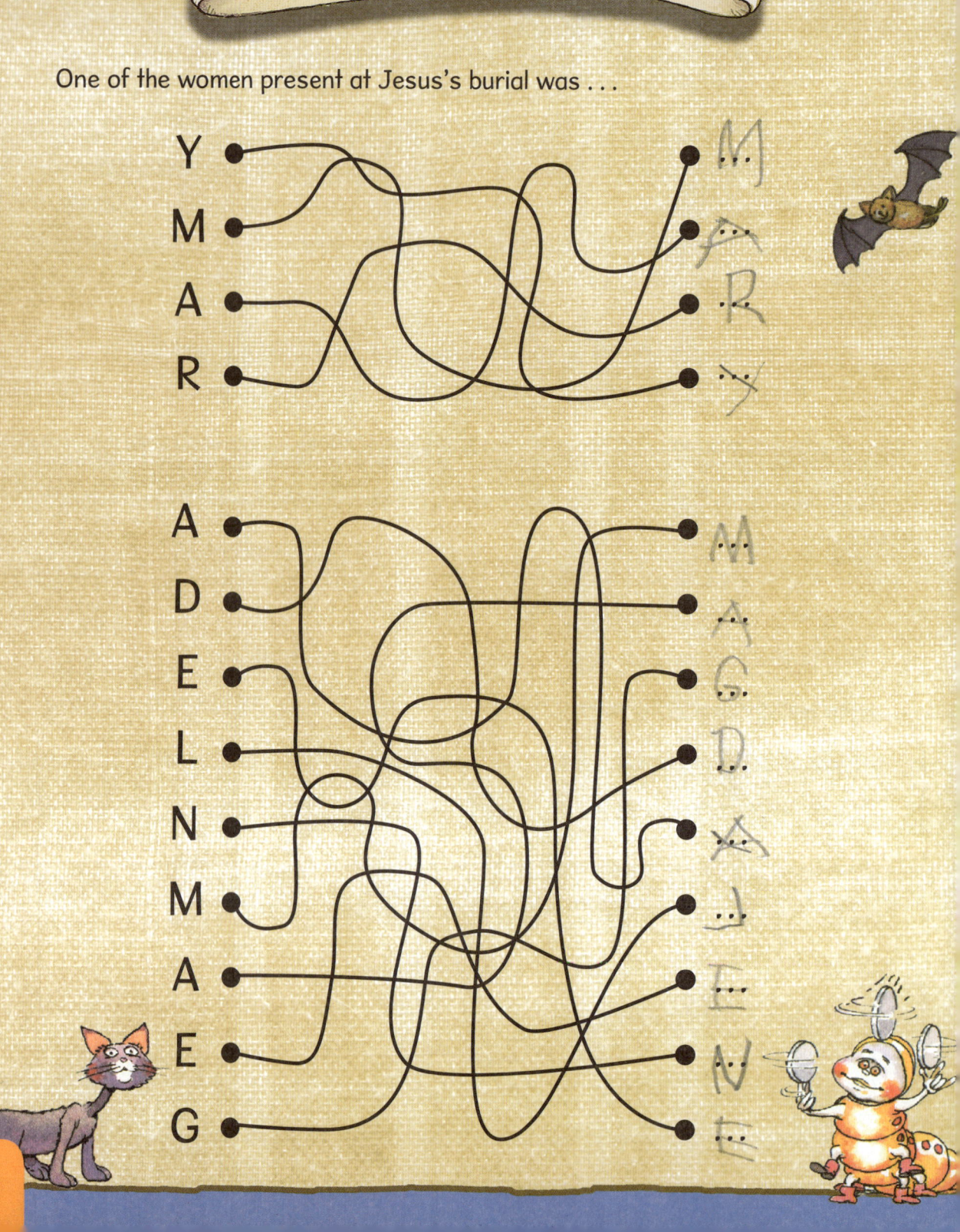

One of the women present at Jesus's burial was . . .

MARY

MAGDALENE

THE BURIAL OF JESUS

Color the picture below of Jesus's friends taking care of Him.

DID YOU KNOW?
The two men who buried Jesus's body were Joseph of Arimathea and Nicodemus. They wrapped Jesus's body in linen with spices according to the Jewish customs and buried it in the tomb that belonged to Joseph.

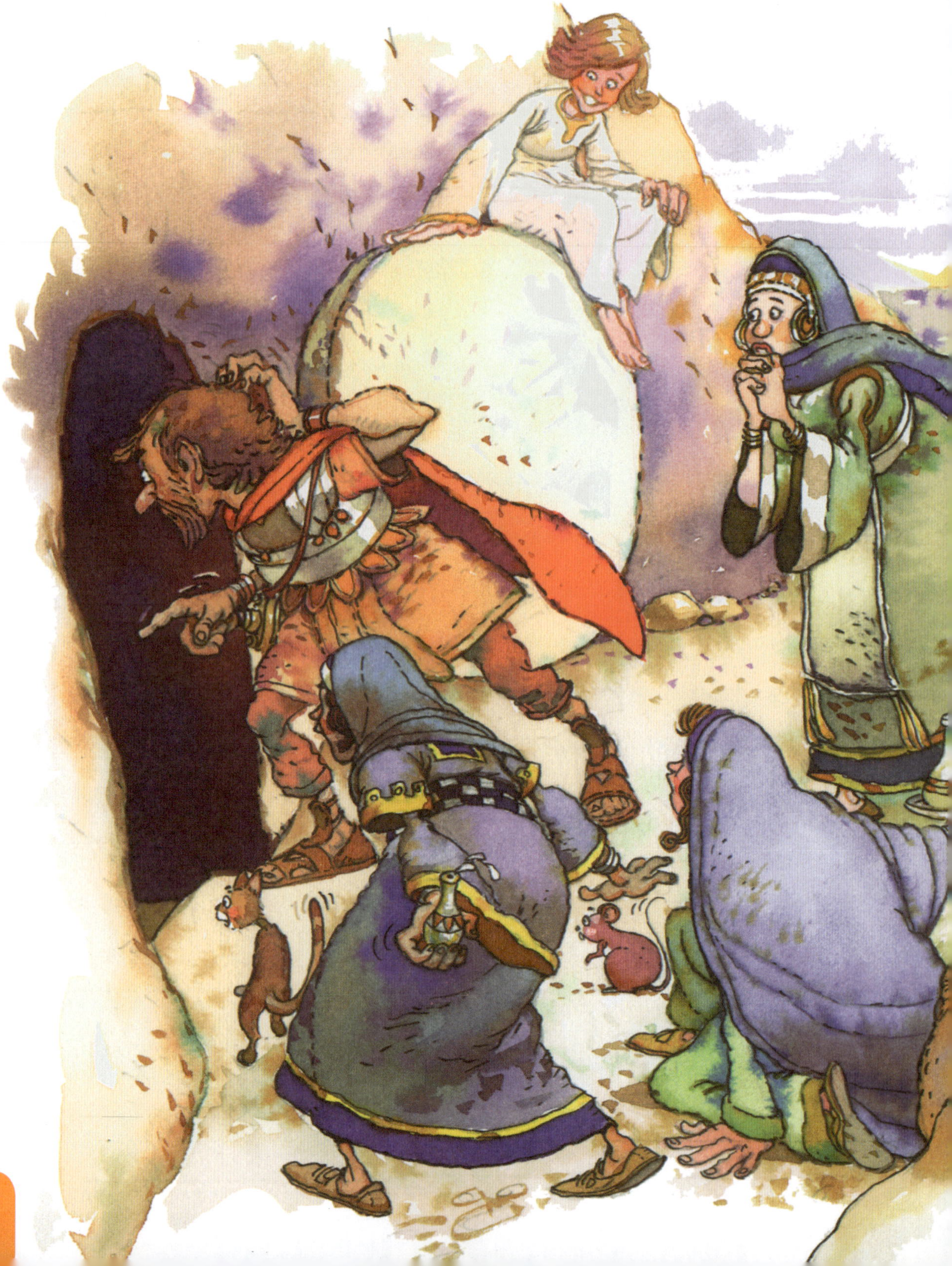

Jesus Is Alive
Matthew 28:1-10

Mary and her friends got up early. It was the third day since Jesus had died. Time to go and visit the cave. The women headed down the road just as the sun began to rise.

All of a sudden, the ground shook. The earth roared. The women could barely keep their balance—it was an *earthquake!* They rushed to the cave.

An angel had rolled away the stone that had covered the entrance to the tomb. And now that shining angel was just sitting on the stone! The guards had fainted.

"Don't be afraid," said the angel. "I know you came to see Jesus. But Jesus is no longer here . . . He is risen and is alive."

"Hi there," said a voice. The three women had been running to tell their friends about the angel. But now someone blocked the road. It was Jesus. "Go tell the others," He said to Mary and her friends. "Tell them I am alive. And that they will soon see Me."

AT THE CAVE

Unscramble the words taken from the story and use the clues to solve the crossword puzzle.

ECAV

NTOSE

VALEI

GALEN

OMWEN

SEUJS

DIRFENS

KERHTAUEQA

word box
ALIVE   FRIENDS
ANGEL   JESUS
CAVE   STONE
EARTHQUAKE   WOMEN

across
1. The messenger sitting on the top of the rock.
2. The _____ made the ground shake.
3. Jesus's _____ went to visit the cave.
4. The angel spoke to the _____.

down
5. The angel rolled the _____ away.
6. _____ is risen.
7. Jesus was buried in a _____.
8. Jesus is not dead, He is _____!

192

MARY MAGDALENE

Look carefully at the pictures of Mary Magdalene. Which two are exactly the same?

1 2 3

4 5 6

DID YOU KNOW?
Mary Magdalene traveled with Jesus as one of his followers. She supported Jesus in his final moments and stayed with him at the cross. She was at his burial, and she was the first person to see Jesus after his resurrection.

194

The Visitor
John 20:19-29

The disciples had just sat down to eat when they heard someone speak. "Peace be with you," said the voice. The disciples looked up from their plates. There, standing in front of them, was Jesus!

Thomas had heard that Jesus had risen and that Mary and the others had seen Him alive after he had been dead. And now Thomas was seeing Jesus for himself.

His friends could see the marks where He was nailed to the cross. Jesus said to Thomas, "Touch me, and believe." Thomas reached out a shaky finger. So—it *was* true! They all laughed and cried, both at the same time.

Jesus had come with a message. "I am giving you a special job," He said to His friends. "I want you to go tell all the people in the world just how much God loves them."

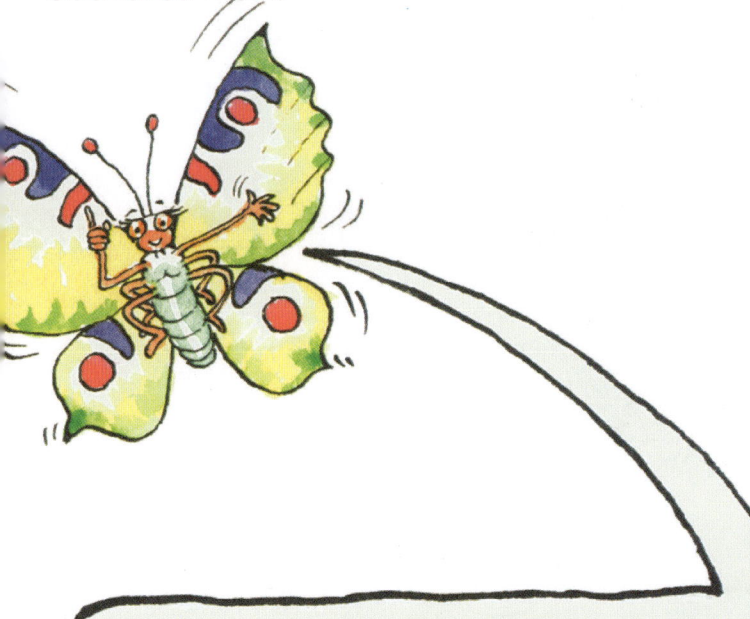

"I am the way, the truth, and the life!" Jesus said. "No one can get to the Father without Me."

DOUBTING THOMAS

Find out where the 5 pictures go and write down the correct number in the space.

DID YOU KNOW?

The disciple Thomas was also known as Didymus (Greek meaning "twin"). But the Bible doesn't tell us who was his twin. After the resurrection of Jesus, he became a great missionary in India.

HAVE FAITH

Use the code to decipher what Jesus said to Thomas.

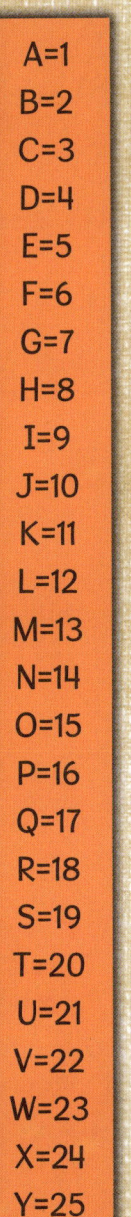

"16 21 20   25 15 21 18   8 1 14 4
 P U T   Y O U R   H A N D

 9 14 20 15   13 25   19 9 4 5
 I N T O   M Y   S I D E

19 20 15 16   4 15 21 2 20 9 14 7
 S T O P   D O U B T I N G

 1 14 4   8 1 22 5
 A N D   H A V E

 6 1 9 20 8 !"
 F A I T H

John 20:27 CEV

Cloud of Heaven
Matthew 28:16-20; John 14:1-3; Acts 1:3-11

It was time for Jesus to go be with God. He gathered His friends on a mountain for a final farewell.

"Once I am gone, wait on God," said Jesus. God was going to pour out His Holy Spirit on them. Then they would be strong for the work to come. His friends still had questions. *Was God going to help their nation?* they wondered. Jesus answered, "It is not for you to know God's time or season." They would get what they needed though; Jesus promised. They were to spread all He had told them to the ends of the earth.

Jesus started to rise up before their eyes. A beautiful cloud picked Him up. Higher and higher, Jesus rose. Then, He was gone. Two men in white appeared among them and said that Jesus would come back again, in the same way He had left.

"In my Father's house are many rooms," Jesus said. "I am going there to make a place for you. One day, I will come again to take you there Myself. So where I live, you will live there too."

FAREWELL

Find 10 differences between these two pictures.

JESUS ROSE UP

Find the 12 hidden words taken from the story of Jesus rising up. They may be up, down, across, backward, or diagonal.

```
F S D N E I R F O G
D A R O O M S A N H
D N R F A E H T M O
U G B E R I E H O U
O E O H W S T E U S
L L M D E E C R N E
C S T C O A L B T C
L O I A J Y V L A A
R A M F O N E E I D
L R E E Z L V H N E
```

WORD BOX

angels	Father	house
cloud	friends	mountain
come	God	time
farewell	heaven	rooms

The Wicked Leader
Acts 8:1-4; 9:1-18

The leader named Saul had enough. Just who did these friends of Jesus think they were anyway? Telling people *who* and *what* to obey. Well, Saul had a way to make them quiet. He was going to arrest each and every last one.

Suddenly, a blast of blinding light made Saul fall from his horse, unable to see. "Saul, Saul . . ." came a voice. "Why do you fight against me?"

"Who are you?" Saul cried. Even with his eyes open, Saul could only see blackness. The mighty leader now felt afraid.

"I am Jesus," said the voice. Jesus told Saul to go into the city and wait. Saul obeyed. His servants led their blind master to where Jesus had said. For three days and nights, Saul did not eat. He did not drink. And he did not see anything but blackness all around him.

At last, the door creaked open. God had sent Ananias to help Saul. Ananias prayed, and Saul could see again. Saul stood up full of joy! He wanted to be baptized right away because Saul had work to do. He was going to tell the whole wide world about Jesus and all the good things of God for those who believed.

Saul was a new man. So he got a new name, too—Paul, a friend of Jesus.

ON THE ROAD TO DAMASCUS

Help Paul find the way to Damascus where he was blinded by the light along the way.

204

A NEW MAN, A NEW NAME

How many times can you find the word PAUL in this grid? It can be up, down, across, backward, and diagonally.

P	A	U	L	
A	A		L	P
U	L	U	A	P
L	A	U	L	
P	L	U	A	P

The word PAUL can be found _____ times.

DID YOU KNOW?
Saul/Paul was born into a Jewish family. His father was a Roman citizen, so he was too. He had 2 names: the Hebrew name Saul and the Latin name Paul. At that time, it was very common to have 2 names. When he began his missionary work to the Gentiles, he started to use his Roman name, Paul.

206

Earthquake at the Jail
Acts 16:16-40

Paul proved how much he loved God. Paul would do whatever it took to spread the good news. *Even* if it meant going to jail. And that is exactly what lay in store for those who tried to change the rules.

Paul and Silas were chained, it was true. Yet their hearts burst with freedom for knowing God's love. The other prisoners heard a song break out. It was Paul and Silas praising God.

Crack! The walls started shaking. *Click*—the cell doors flew open as if by themselves. With a great loud *clank,* their chains all dropped to the ground.

The prison guard was terrified. What must he do—he begged to know—to be *saved?* Paul and Silas were happy to help. "Just believe in Jesus," they told him. The guard invited them to his house to have a bath and a meal. Then Paul and Silas baptized him and all his family.

IN PRISON

Find out the 2 mystery words by filling in the missing letter of each vertical word. There are extra words in the word box that don't fit.

	H	L	J	L	G	S	S	W
	O	O	A	A	O	O	E	O
→	P	R	I	S	O	N	E	R
	E	D	L	T	D	G	K	K

	H	B	B	S	S	E	G	S	S	F
→	E	A	R	T	H	Q	U	A	K	E
	A	T	E	O	A	U	A	V	I	A
	R	H	A	N	K	I	R	E	L	R
	T	E	K	E	E	P	D	D	L	S

word box:
BATHE
BREAK
ENJOY
EQUIP
FEARS
FROWN
GOOD
GUARD
HEART
HOPE
JAIL
JOIN
LAST
LORD
SAVED
SEEK
SHAKE
SKILL
SONG
STONE
WAIT
WORK

OUT OF JAIL

Find the right path from the prison to the guard's house.

The Shipwreck
Acts 27–28

Paul was in chains . . . again. He had not obeyed orders. He had not stopped teaching about Jesus. So now Paul was put on a ship to sail for a distant land.

Things at sea were looking dark. A mighty storm howled as huge waves splashed the deck. The sailors were certain they were all going to die . . . when their prisoner stood up.

Paul had something to say. "Don't be afraid," said Paul. He had dreamed of an angel who was keeping watch. "God is going to save each and every one of us," Paul told the crew.

There were few other choices but to take Paul at his word. He said there was no need to save food. The sailors watched Paul take a huge bite of bread. Then they all joined in. At least they could enjoy a final feast before the storm sank their ship.

Just then—what was that on the horizon? An island! Paul and the crew swam for shore. The friendly island people built a fire while Paul told about Jesus. When they were ready to set sail, Paul and the sailors said goodbye to their new friends and kept sailing to Rome.

When they finally got to Rome, Paul was guarded by soldiers, but he still boldly taught about the Lord Jesus Christ to anyone who came to see him.

ON THE BOAT

Paul traveled on a ship. Use the grid to help you draw one, square by square. Then, color it!

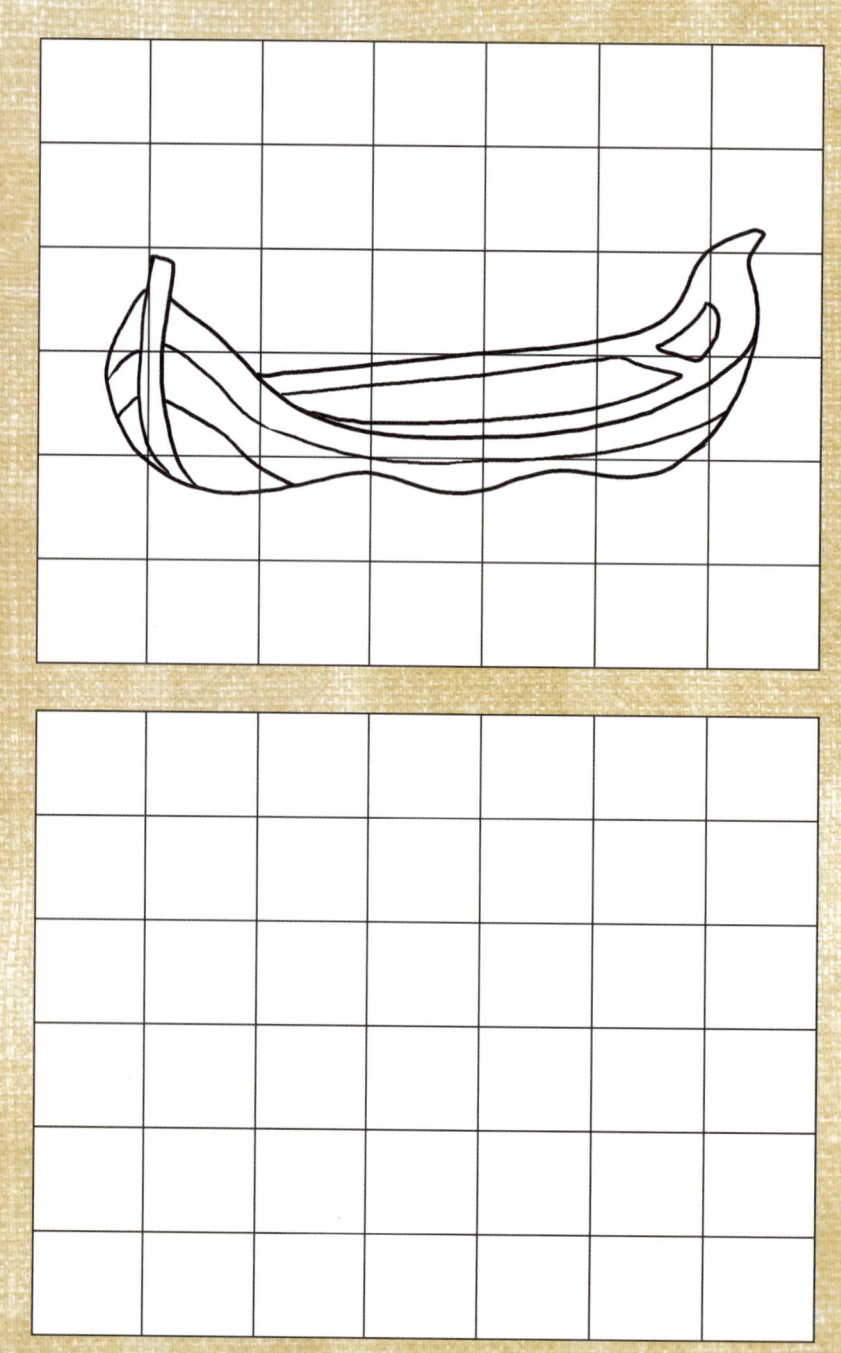

SAFE ON THE ISLAND

Complete the patterns and find out the name of the island.

P-R-Y-M-P-R-Y-M-P-R-Y- (M)

Z-I-I-A-Z-I-I-A-Z-I-I- (a)

U-L-U-K-U-L-U-K-U- (L)

O-T-T-O-T-T-O-T-T-O- (t)

H-E-G-A-H-E-G-A-H-E-G- (a)

The name is: malta.

DID YOU KNOW?
Paul went on many missionary journeys after he became a believer, including three long missionary journeys throughout the Roman Empire.

213

The World to Come
Micah 4:3-4; Revelation 1, 21

John dreamed that one day, Jesus will come again. On that day, all wars will end. Weapons will be turned into garden tools. Each person will sit under their own tree in peace.

On that day, all things will be made new. Those who believe will see Jesus at last. And people from every nation will sing out in joy.

And John told everything that he had seen about God's message and about what Jesus Christ had said and done.

JOHN'S DREAM

Find 16 crabs hidden in the picture below.

ABOUT REVELATION

Revelation was written by John, the apostle who had been one of Jesus's disciples. While he was held on a prison island called Patmos, John received a vision from Jesus. He wrote what he saw in this book that we call Revelation, the last book of the Bible.

JESUS WILL COME BACK

Decipher an important verse from the book of Revelation using the code below.

✳ = A	❖ = I	⊖ = U
⌘ = E	⊠ = O	

Th_ L_rd G_d s_ys, "_ _m _lph_ _nd _m_g_, th_ _n_ wh_ _s _nd w_s _nd _s c_m_ng. _ _m G_d _ll-P_w_rf_l!"

Revelation 1:8 CEV

How many words can you make with the letters from REVELATION?

_____

_____

_____

_____

_____

_____

217

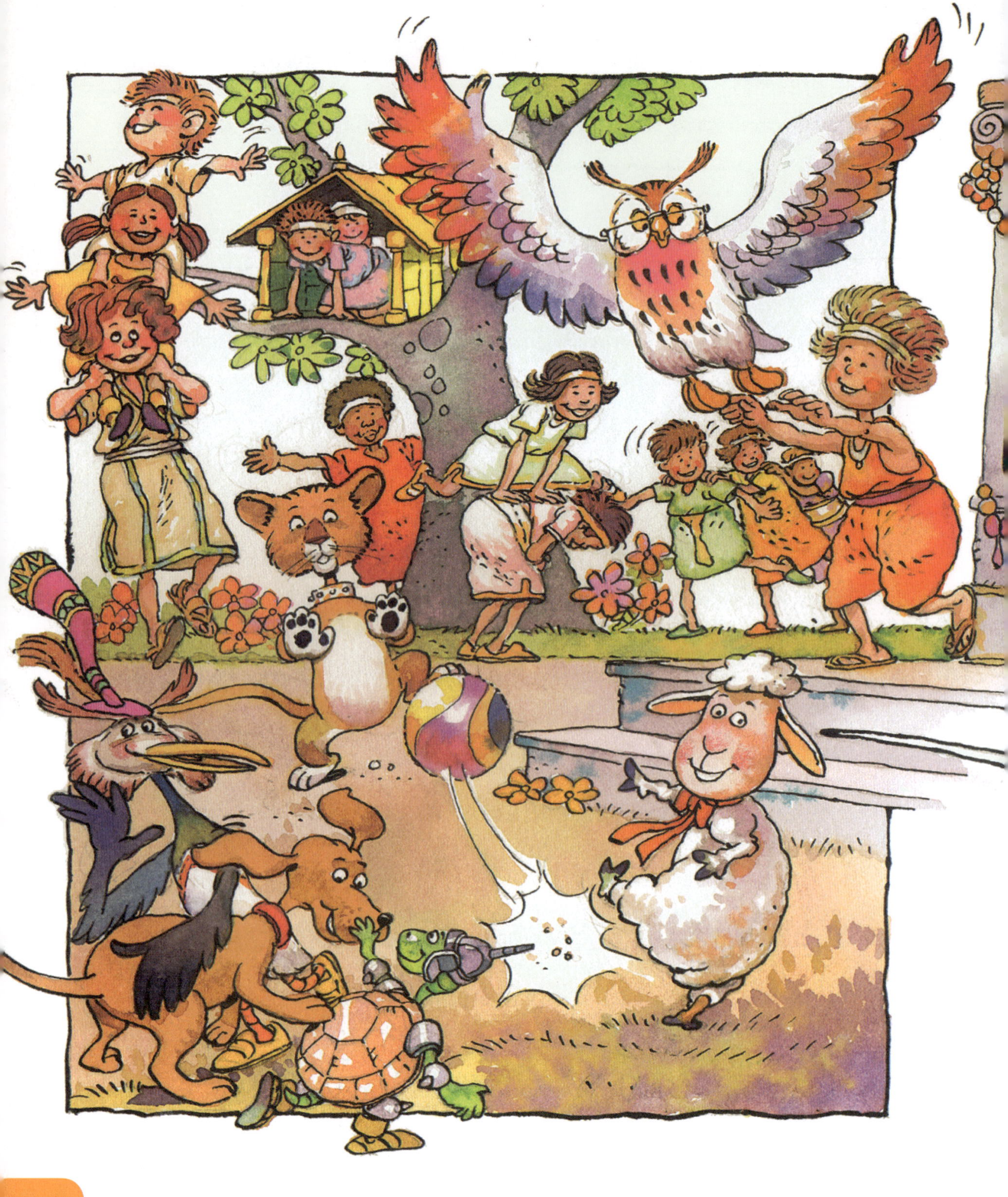

The Promise
Revelation 21

In heaven God will wipe away all our tears. For those who trusted in Jesus and lived for Him on Earth, there will be no more sadness. There will be no pain. But those who did not believe and did wrong on earth shall be sent away.

In heaven there will be no sun or moon. Heaven will shine bright with the glory of God. Jesus will be our light. The streets will be gold. The gates will be pearls. People from everywhere will sing of God's goodness. And believers will live in joy forever and ever.

"I am the beginning," says God, "and I am the end. I was there at the first, and I will be there at the last."

GOD'S GOODNESS

Can you find 10 differences between the two pictures?

LIVING IN JOY

Make your very own illustration of heaven. You can use markers, glitter, collage . . .

REMEMBER

The only way to heaven is through Jesus. Jesus forgives our sins when we ask Him for forgiveness and invite Him into our hearts.

GAME SOLUTIONS

THE OLD TESTAMENT

(pages 10-11) In the Beginning
Unscramble: Mars, Neptune, Uranus, Jupiter, Venus, Earth, Mercury, Saturn

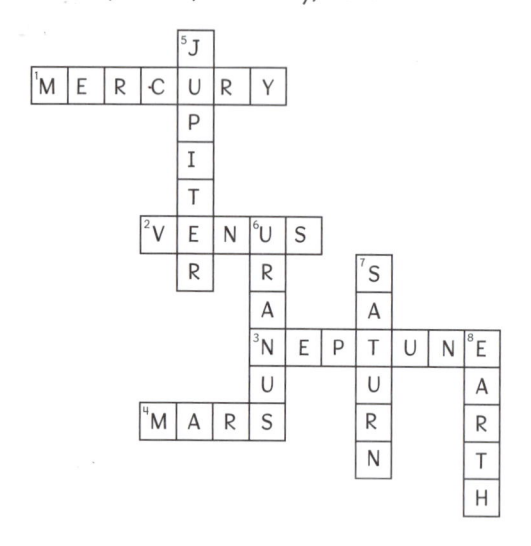

Planets' positions (from top to bottom): Venus, Mercury, Earth, Mars, Jupiter, Neptune, Saturn, Uranus

(pages 14-15) God Brings Life
Penguin number 6 is the one that is different.

God makes the animals: earth, fish, birds, animals.

Animals and birds:
1. dolphin, zebra, horse, rabbit
2. donkey, chicken, beaver, camel
3. snake, panda, ostrich, penguin
4. tiger, peacock, seagull, turtle

(pages 18-19) Adam and Eve

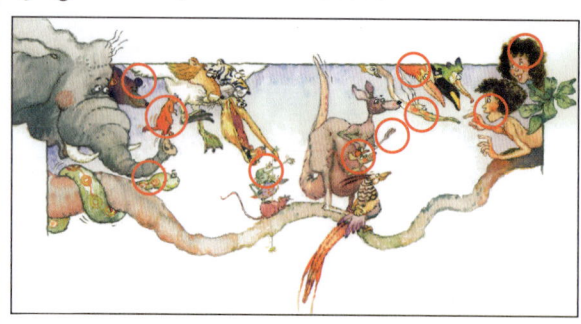

(pages 22-23) Two Brothers
The word is SACRIFICE.

The word *lamb* can be found 8 times.

222

(pages 26-27) God Calls on Noah

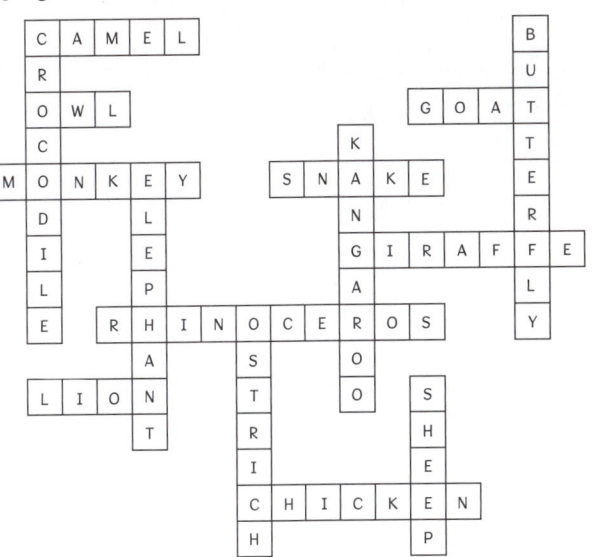

(pages 30-31) The Great Flood
Boats: sailboat and rowboat

There are 10 boats in the drawing.

Story quiz: 1. 40 days; 2. A dove

(pages 34-35) Promise in a Rainbow

(pages 38-39) The Tower of Babel
The word is LOVING.

Tower 2 is different.

(pages 42-43) Abraham and Sarah

223

Synonyms: land/country; shelter/camp; promise/vow; trust/faith; desert/wilderness.

(pages 46-47) Abraham's Great Big Family
SARAH was the wife of Abraham.
ISAAC was the only son Abraham and Sarah had.
JACOB was the son of Isaac and Rebekah.
ABRAHAM is the "father of many nations."

(pages 50-51) A Coat of Many Colors

Unscramble: "When Joseph came to his brothers, they pulled off his fancy coat."

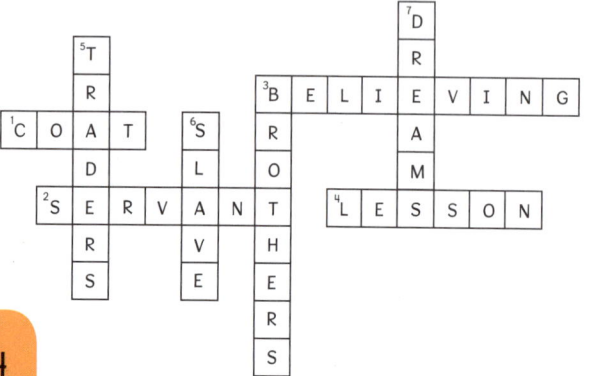

Crossword:
1. COAT
2. SERVANT
3. BELIEVING
4. LESSON
5. TRADERS
6. SLEEVE
7. DREAM
Down: BROTHERS

(pages 54-55) The Faith of Joseph

Shadow number 1 belongs to Joseph.
Joseph's family: Benjamin

(pages 58-59) The Baby in a Basket

Baby Moses 3 is different.

(pages 62-63) The Burning Bush
Running away: Moses ran to hide in a region called MIDIAN. There he married a woman named Zipporah and became a SHEPHERD, and took care of many ANIMALS.

224

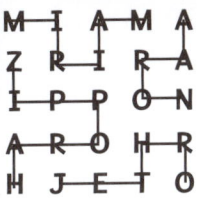

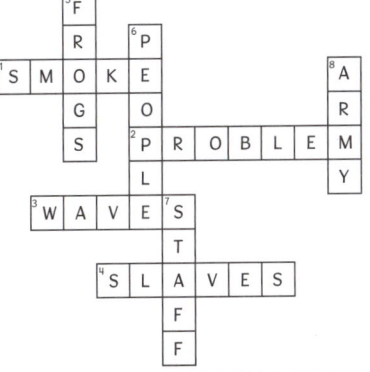

(pages 70-71) The Promised Land
Becoming a leader: "I've commanded you to be strong and brave."

(pages 66-67) Journey Through the Sea
Out of Egypt: frogs, people, slaves, smoke, staff, army, problem, waves

(pages 74-75) Gideon Wants Proof
The answers are: soldier 2, camel 4, and soldier 1.

(pages 78-79) Samson the Strong
Dot-to-dot: a lion.

225

Samson's strength:
1. strong, courageous, supernatural, powerful
2. robust, capable, vigorous, solid

(pages 82-83) Ruth's Reward

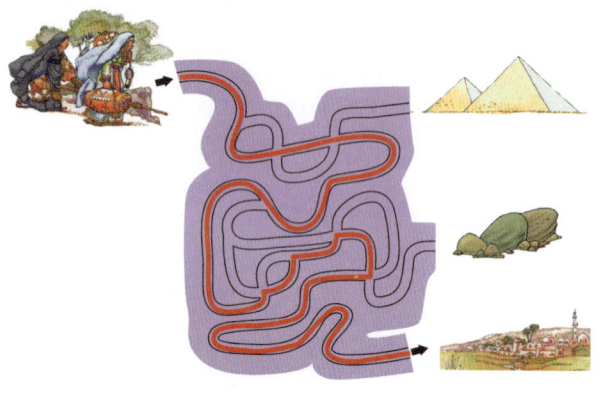

Loyalty: "Your people will be my people. Your God will be my God."

(pages 86-87) The Shepherd Boy
The shape is a bear.
Shadow 3 matches the shape.

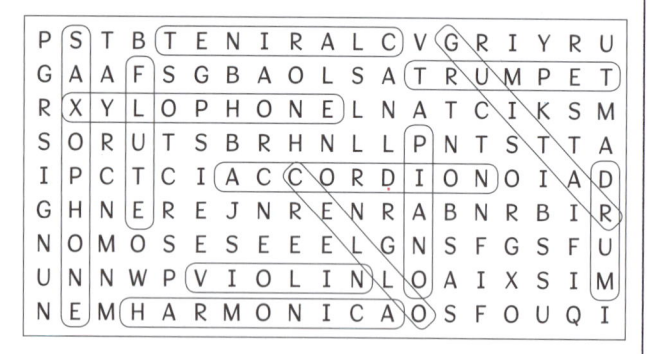

(pages 90-91) David and Goliath

(pages 94-95) The Wisest King

Shadow number 2 belongs to the man holding the baby.

Facts about God's temple: In the FOURTH year of his reign, Solomon began the CONSTRUCTION of the Temple. SEVEN years later it was completed, and the ARK of the COVENANT was moved to the Temple.

(pages 98-99) Elijah the Prophet
The answers are: bread, famine, ravens, brook, message, woman, prophet, flour.

(pages 102-103) Esther, Brave and Fair
There are 17 overlapping crowns.

Esther's uncle: Mordecai.

(pages 106-107) The Lions' Den

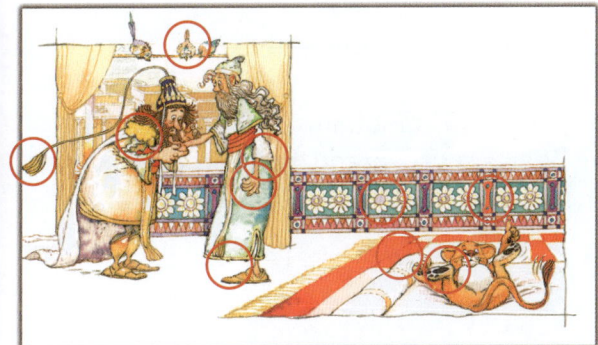

(pages 110-111) Jonah and the Whale
The sea creature that is not a fish is:

THE NEW TESTAMENT
(pages 116-117) Mary and Joseph
Shadow number 2 belongs to the angel.

Story quiz:
1. Angel Gabriel
2. She was going to give birth to God's only Son.
3. Joseph also had a visit from an angel, who explained to Joseph what was going to happen.

(pages 120-121) A King Is Born
The nativity story: "Praise God in heaven! Peace on earth to everyone who pleases God."

(pages 124-125) Three Wise Men

The wise men's gifts: 1 • C; 2 • A; 3 • B

(pages 128-129) Fishers of Men

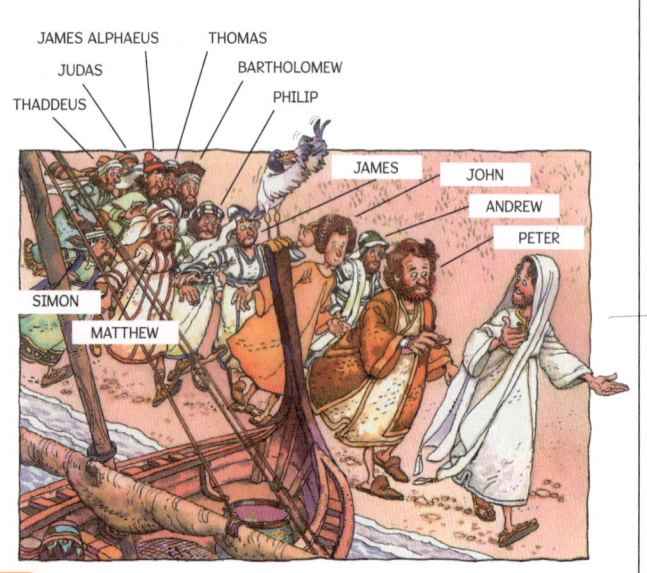

Following Jesus: "JESUS said to them, "COME with me! I will TEACH you how to BRING in people instead of FISH."

Color the dots: a fish.

(pages 132-133) Love Your Enemy

(pages 136-137) The Loving Father
Pictures 3 and 4 are exactly the same.

A forgiving father: "But we should be glad and celebrate! Your brother was dead, but he is now alive."

(pages 140-141) Water into Wine

The true vine: branches.

There are 9 overlapping jars.

(pages 144-145) The Miracles of Jesus
Jesus's miracles: "GET UP! Pick up your MAT and go on HOME".

The miracles are: Jesus turned water into wine, drove out evil spirits, healed the sick, raised to life, calmed the storm.

(pages 148-149) The Great Storm

Calming the storm: still, disciples, peace, power, storm, drown, waves, wind.

			P	E	A	C	E	
			O					
		D	R	O	W	N		
		I		E				
W		S	T	O	R	M		
A		C						
V		I						
E		W	I	N	D			
S	T	I	L	L				
		E						
		S						

(pages 152-153) The Endless Feast
Loaves and fish: 2 fish and 5 loaves

(pages 156-157) Back from the Dead

229

(pages 160-161) **Jesus Walks on Water**

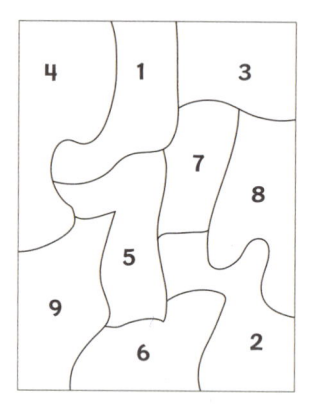

Jesus's miraculous power: "The men in the boat worshipped Jesus and said, 'You really are the Son of God.'"

(pages 164-165) **Let the Children Come**
Picture 2 is different.

Jesus's words are: "If you want to be GREAT, you must be the SERVANT of all the OTHERS."

(pages 168-169) **Hosanna to the King**

Shadow 2 belongs to Jesus on the donkey.

(pages 172-173) **The Last Supper**

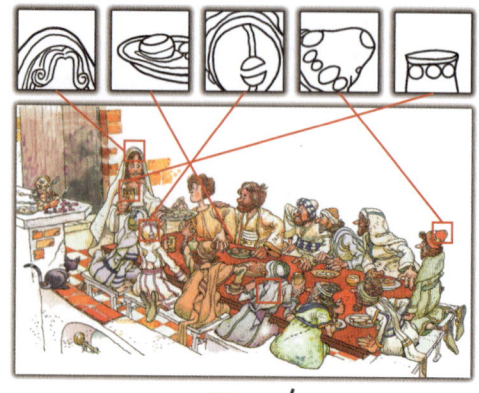

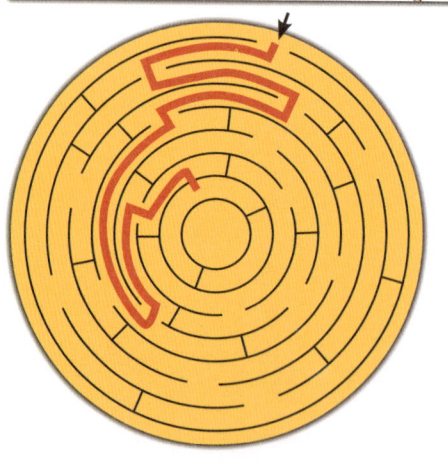

(pages 176-177) Soldiers at the Garden Gate

(pages 180-181) Peter Lies About Jesus

Silhouette 5 matches Peter.

Memory game: 1. Two; 2. One; 3. A man pointing at Peter; 4. Jesus

(pages 184-185) The Cross on the Hill

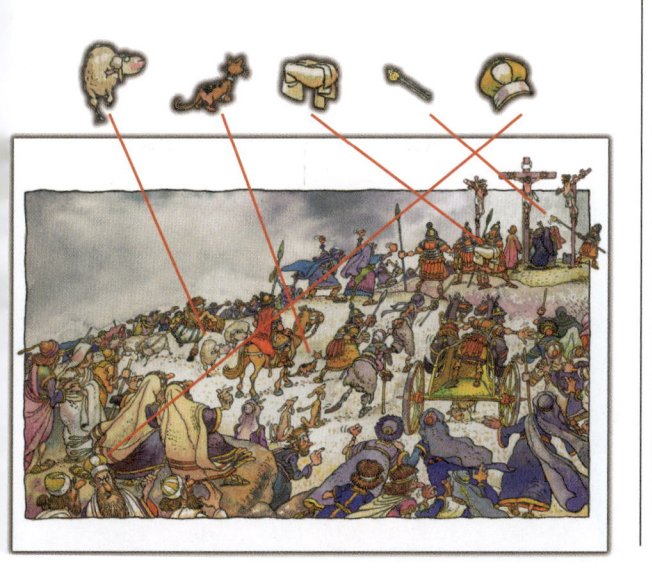

Jesus died for our sins: "GOD loved the PEOPLE of this world SO MUCH that he gave his only SON, so that EVERYONE who has FAITH in him will have ETERNAL life and never really DIE."

There are 11 overlapping crosses.

(pages 188-189) A Cave for a King
One of the women present at Jesus's burial was Mary Magdalene.

(pages 192-193) Jesus Is Alive
The answers are: cave, stone, alive, angel, women, Jesus, friends, earthquake.

The pictures of Mary Magdalene 2 and 4 are exactly the same.

(pages 196-197) The Visitor

231

Have faith: "Put your hand into my side. Stop doubting and have faith!"

(pages 200-201) Cloud of Heaven

(pages 204-205) The Wicked Leader

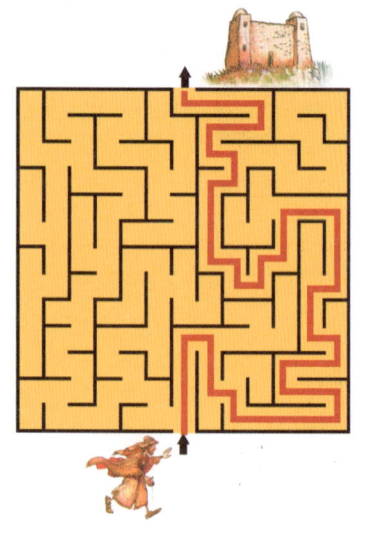

The word *Paul* can be found 7 times.

(pages 208-209) Earthquake at the Jail
The 2 mystery words are: prisoner, earthquake.

Out of jail: The right path is 1.

(pages 212-213) The Shipwreck
The name of the island is Malta.

(pages 216-217) The World to Come

Jesus will come back: "The Lord God says, "I am alpha and omega, the one who is and was and is coming. I am God all-powerful!"

Some of the words you can make with the letters from "REVELATION": alive, are, elevation, elevator, eternal, in, interval, late, later, lean, lion, live, love, not, note, on, rail, rain, rant, rat, rate, rave, real, relate, relative, relevant, reveal, tail, tailor, tale, tan, tine, ton, tone, trail, train, trainee, tree, trial, vale, veal, vial

(pages 220-221) The Promise

232